Creative Techniques for Wearables

Love & best wishes to Jeanne —
Jenny

by
Jenny Raymond

Thanks

To my daughter Mary Karol McGee, who helped edit this book. Her knowledge and understanding was amazing, thank you MK for your assistance in this project.

Dedicated

To my husband Bob for his support, I could not do all I am doing with it. He has been my partner in life for over 42 years, thank you for being such a caring and thoughtful man.

Acknowledgments

The Sewing Basket - The fabric store I had for nine years where I received my "College" degree in Business, Management, Merchandising and Wearable Design.

My love and appreciation goes to…………………..

My mom, **Mary Edna Cooper** of Waco, Texas, for allowing me to play with scraps at her feet as a child and for patiently teaching a little girl who so desperately wanted to learn to sew.

My sister, **Karol Blakey** of Waco, Texas, for being the best sister ever, my "personal shopper" and one of my best friends.

My children, **Jeff, Mary Karol and Sara**, who suffered through years of wearing "Mom's Creations" and to my new children **Craig**, Mary Karol's husband and **Julie**, Jeff's wife.

The newest stars on our family tree, **MaKayla Dawn Raymond**, our first grandchild was born May 9, 2003. Second granddaughter, **Madeline Kate (Maddie) McGee**, was born April 7, 2004. Now I understand that special love that we have for our grandbabies. Wow…..these little girls have captured my heart!

The friends, I love………………………..

Linda Goad, who does not sew a stitch, but is a constant source of encouragement and love to me.

Brenda Kincaid, my faithful Nebraska quilter friend. The question "what can I do to help" is always on her lips.

Kay Figart, of Conroe, TX. Her gift of hospitality goes without speaking.

The **many friends** from all over the country that have given me friendship and the desire to continue doing what I do.

Thanks to the following for their permission to mention their work……….
Libby Lehman   Catherine Anthony   Larkin Van Horn
Ilaine Hartman   Linda Dean   Marcia Kaylakie
Stephanie Goddard   Joanne Hansen   Joyce Landorf Heatherley   Diane Womack of Arkansas

Photography - K & D Photography, Gothenburg, Nebr. Donnis Hueftle-Bullock.
Photos by Perrault Studios and courtesy of Quilts, Inc., Jeff and Jenny Raymond.

Printed by Morgantown Printing and Binding, Morgantown, WV 26508

Additional copies of this book may be ordered from Jenny Raymond, 817 23rd St., Gothenburg, NE 69138. $28.00 each book, NE residents add $1.96 for sales tax plus $4.00 for shipping and handling.

Table of Contents . . . .

Notes........Your ideas.............from the Internet..........

Preface. . . . .

I'm writing this so that you will know my heart and who I am. It's the nice thing about self-publishing a book,
you can write and include what you want. I'm not a writer, just someone whose head is filled with thoughts, ideas and designs.
I wanted to share them with you. If you're wondering how it all came about, read the following.
We all have an experience in life that makes a difference, changes us forever - my life has been no different.

Summer 2004
Dear "Sisters and Brothers of the Cloth":

Garment making has been a part of my life for as long as I can remember. I started making doll clothes by hand when I was in the first grade. I had no patterns; so I make up my own and used the scraps from the dresses our mother made for my sister Karol and I.

I don't remember a time when I did not want to sew. There wasn't a 4-H program in Waco, Texas where I grew up so I didn't have the benefit of their fine efforts with young people. My mother didn't think I was old enough to use the sewing machine until I was in the seventh grade so everything before then was sewn by hand. No wonder, I don't like hand sewing.

When I was a young girl I would fantasize about having my own sewing machine, dreaming that I might enter a contest and win the prize of a sewing machine. I just wanted to sew. Mother never had to drag me into the fabric store as I always enjoyed feeling fabric. The basic principles of sewing that I learned from Mother were to always fit the garment and press open my seams. I didn't like to press open seams: it took too much time! It wasn't long before I realized this was one reason my projects didn't always turn out well. After that, I listened to my Mama.

I finally started using Mom's straight stitch Singer and I thought I was in heaven. Mom taught me the basics of sewing and I finally had lessons in ninth grade Home Economics. The first dress I made was a sleeveless sheath and short jacket in mint green for Easter, ala 1959.

Bob Raymond of Cozad, NE traveled to Texas in the fall of 1961 to escape the cold and to attend Baylor University for one year. He was two years out of high school, and had been raised on a farm in central Nebraska where they raised grain crops and fed live stock. I was a senior in high school that year and we met at the church my family attended, First Methodist Church. Our first date was right before Thanksgiving and it lasted twelve hours. We went to a Baylor football game, out to eat and then to a movie. I was impressed, he was cute, very nice and he treated me like gold. We dated that year and he asked me to marry him before

the Easter break. I told him, I'd let him know when he got back from Nebraska. If I remember correctly he drove from Cozad, NE to Waco, TX in 11 hours. That was 850 miles on two lane highways, many years before the interstate system. I said yes and before long we were engaged. That August my mother and I visited Nebraska for the first time.

On November 24, 1962, Virginia Ruth Cooper and Robert Charles Raymond were united in marriage at the First United Methodist Church in Waco. We moved to Cozad, Nebraska where he farmed with his dad. I was 18 and Bob was 21.

The following February, he bought me my first sewing machine. At last I had my own machine. Wow! It was a Singer, my mother had a Singer, so I thought that was the machine I should have. It did not have a lot of features but I was thrilled with it. I made curtains for our apartment and dresses for our nieces the second Christmas we were married. Most of what I sewed was by the "seat of my pants", but when a technique was learned, it was learned well.

Farming did not work out well for us so Bob returned to Baylor in the fall of 1964. I worked during those college years and earned my PHT (Put Hubby Through) degree as did many young wives of those years. Bob graduated from Baylor University Cum Laude in 1967. We moved to Denver where he went to work for, at that time, one of the top accounting firms in the world, Arthur Anderson.

I was pregnant with our first child and our son Jeff was born in December of 1967. We bought a brick ranch home and settled into suburban life. I had a new job in life, that of being a mom and it was one I loved. We had a darling blue eyed, red headed son.

The following spring, Bob bought me my dream machine, the Singer Touch and Sew. I must admit I liked the feature of filling the bobbin in the bobbin casing; it filled a need for a number of years.

About that time, I decided I was tired of being poor. Bob was right out of college and there were school loans to repay, a new mortgage, new baby, and no insurance for his birth, etc. etc. I decided to see if I could build a business sewing for the public. I placed an advertisement on the bulletin board at an area laundry mat.

The first person to respond was a young bride to be and she wanted me to make her dress and veil. Oh boy! I never made anything like that before. It was so... so involved. I said yes because I had to start some place. With lots of work on my part, the dress turned very well. Thank goodness the styles were simple at that time.

My clientele grew and so did my skills. I'll never forget the princess style coat pattern a woman brought to me. Can you guess what kind of fabric she purchased? A plaid. Oh my....I'd never sewn with plaid fabric before, at least not when they had to be matched. What a learning experience that coat was. The plaid match turned out perfectly, even the sleeves. After that, matching plaids became a passion for me. It's one thing at which I am very good.

In January of 1970, we moved from Denver to San Francisco. What an experience for two young people living in the heart of that fabulous city in a high rise apartment. We were three blocks from the financial district where Bob worked and three blocks from China Town. I'm glad we had that opportunity for many reasons but one very important reason was shopping at Britex Fabrics.

We soon found out California life was not for us. We decided that we wanted to raise our son in an different environment. Our California friends thought we were crazy, moving to where? Nebraska? Is that on this continent? We chose to live in Gothenburg, 10 miles down the road from Cozad.

It was the best decision we ever made in our life. We started our own CPA firm and Bob jokingly says, he didn't make enough money the first year to pay his secretary. Needless to say, that situation has changed. He's worked hard and has been very successful as a CPA.

After settling in Gothenburg, I decided to start sewing again and this I did for 30 years. My only regret is that I didn't keep a journal of all the garments I made. The bridesmaids, prom, bridal gowns, every day clothing; the numbers, styles, and colors would be unbelievable.

During the 80's I had the "Sewing Basket", a full-line fabric store in Gothenburg. Those years were wonderful years of growth for me. My confidence and knowledge grew by leaps and bounds. I loved going to Kansas City for market twice a year; I still miss those times today. In my store, I could "feel" and love each bolt of fabric - for me it was heaven on earth!

I tried every creative idea possible to make the business work. After struggling to survive for 9 years, like so many small business, I closed the doors. It took so much energy, time and money. I never missed any of our children's activities, as I had good help, but I couldn't do it any longer. The bills were always paid and I had a good inventory. In nine years I never gave myself a salary and I paid for everything I took out of it. I wanted it to succeed more than anything.

My need to be home for the kids was greater than my need to have the store. It closed in March of 1989. Even today, women tell me how much they miss it. I made so many friends, taught so many classes and learned so much. Bob was kind and gracious to let it be a part of my life. I would not be doing what I do today, if it had not been for the store. May I tell you how it all came to be?

When Jeff was four, our daughter Mary Karol was born. I finally had a girl for whom to sew. She was a blond with the biggest blue eyes you have ever seen. This was the best - a girl, I loved ruffles, but from the get go Mary Karol didn't like ruffles! I tried to convert her to my way of thinking but to no avail. I finally realized she would rather play outside than dress in ruffles. She won!

In May of 1977, another daughter Angela Ruth was born. With three great children, I had my tubes tied after her birth. What a sweet baby she was, ash blond hair and blue eyes. Another little girl to sew for; until that tragic day July 30, 1978 when she died in a drowning accident at Jeffrey Lake south of Brady, Nebraska where we have a lake home. Thank God, the accident was at a neighbor's home and not ours - what heartache, tears and growth lay ahead for me.

There were times I didn't think I could make it another day, my heart hurt so bad. I was raised in a Christian home and for that I am eternally grateful, but I had strayed from that precious faith through the years and God used Angie's death to draw me back and he did it in a way I would have never imagined.

After her death I found I didn't even know where to look in the Bible for comfort. Through His mercy that has changed over the years because of a good church home and wonderful pastors.

Because I have always been a reader, I went to a book store searching for a book that might help. I found one, two years before the writing of the book, the author lost her son to leukemia. According to the book, after those two years, she was still in despair and had no hope. She couldn't function as a wife and mother to her other children. I was so broken with grief, I knew that if I was in the same state I was then after two years, I would probably be dead, I couldn't endure the pain that long.

Soon after, I went to a Christian book store and found a little book that helped change my life. It was "Mourning Song" by Joyce Landorf Heatherley. One passage in her book has stayed with me over all these many years:

We may all find ourselves in the place of not knowing or understanding the whys of death, There is so much in this world we don't understand or know, so it is not a question of having all the answers at our fingertips, but rather entrusting to God our painful whys and then watching His quiet peace erase the fear, bitterness and frustrations from the blackboards of our minds.

This passage ministered to me day after day and in time I knew that my heart would sing again. God was showing me that the only way to heal was to let Him be the healer

I could no longer have children so we decided to try and adopt a baby. In September I went to my OB, Dr. Bernie Taylor in No. Platte, Nebraska. Several years before he and his wife had lost a little daughter to brain cancer, so I knew he would understand my pain. Over the years Dr. Taylor had placed many babies in homes, he promised to put us on his list, but said it could be a year and a half. The first of December I had a *"knowing"* that I was going to have another baby. My periods were regular, but the *knowing feeling* was so strong, so real.

Time went on until the day after Christmas. I was washing noon dishes and the phone rang. I answered and a male voice said "are you still in the mothering mood?" It was Dr. Taylor. There was a baby was due January 8th. He asked if we would be interested in having this baby I couldn't believe it, so soon after Angie's death, it was a miracle. Somehow, I *knew* in my heart of hearts, this was going to happen. We said yes and on January 8th our daughter Sara Marie Raymond was born. We brought her home on January 10th to a town of friends filled with good wishes and tears. Needless to say, the grief process had not played it self out.

That spring we decided to build a new home and that project kept my mind occupied. I was a busy mom, keeping up with Jeff, MK and Sara (not counting the dogs and cats) filled my days. Seventeen months later in October of 1980, we moved into our new home.

That winter the local dime store that carried everything from hardware to fabrics closed. Bob thought maybe it was the time for me to realize a long time dream and open a fabric store. I'll always feel there was another reason for his encouragement to open my own business, he was trying to find ways to help me heal after Angie's death. Her death had shaken me to the very foundation of my being. Still today her death can come on like a storm because I never saw her grow up. In my eyes she's still a 14 month old toddler, dependent upon her mother.

Because of Bob's love for me, all the good things connected to my sewing have happened. I believe with all my heart; if the Sewing Basket had never existed, I wouldn't be doing in life what I'm doing today.

After it closed and I had time, I joined the Nebraska State Quilt Guild. I saw other quilter's teaching and some were becoming very successful at their work. I wondered if I worked hard enough, I could teach myself. During the SB years, I taught classes, worked with Bishop sewing groups, and judged Make it with Wool contest. My sewing skills were very good, so I had a lot of good experience to share.

That fall after the store closed a sewing guild in Kearney, NE called and wanted me to present a program on bridal sewing. I knew that it took hours to prepare a new lecture or workshop and that I would never have a need for a bridal presentation. I thought.....maybe... oh what the heck, it won't hurt to ask......would they be interested in a program on creative techniques for wearables? They said yes and the rest is history.

Each July, the Nebraska State Quilt Guild has its yearly conference, QuiltNebraska. This is my weekend with the girls, seeing people who have greatly influenced my life. Each year I would make new garments to wear. One of my garments would be my challenge piece for QN. During that time of my life; I was challenging myself more and more, and my work was improving. So were my teaching skills. I'll never forget the first year I was asked to teach for QN, I was elated. At that point in my life this was like being asked to teach at Quilt Festival.

The changing point in my sewing came at Quilt Nebraska 1993 in Hastings, NE. For the challenge, I made a jacket and skirt with mariners compass stars on the jacket. It was striking! Paulette Peters, a great friend who was teaching on the national circuit at that time, came to me and said "Jenny, I think you should send in a portfolio for the Fairfield Fashion Show. Oh my...I knew about the FFS, because several times it was presented at market back in the 80's It was a show for people who were the best in their field - big names like Virginia Avery. Me try? Oh dear!!!!

Her encouragement was all I needed. I asked friends how to put together a portfolio. I set up a photo session with our local photographer and she shot great pictures of my best three ensembles. Eight pictures were carefully arranged in a photo portfolio and in early November I mailed it to Fairfield.

I was excited, but realistic. I knew one way or the other, I would get a letter. Fairfield would be kind enough to respond. I was told I would hear by the end of January.

On January 26, 1994, I went to the mailbox and there was a big stack of mail. I shuffled down through the stack and on the bottom was a letter from Fairfield. I opened it on the spot and it said "Congratulations..." I spent that day crying, hyperventilating, and calling my friends and family. It was one of the best days of my life.

One skill I worked hard at developing, was fussy cutting and piecing very involved star blocks. This was the technique I wanted to use for my first outfit. Large sheets of graph paper were taped together to draw the design for the jacket and the skirt. After several hundred hours of work, "Starlight Rhapsody" was completed and photographed. I mailed it by the deadline in August.

I was nervous as a cat. Would Fairfield like it? Would I embarrass my self at the show beside all the other designers? I would not have the answers until the night of the first showing at Quilt Market in November. A friend from Nebraska had a booth at Quilt Market that year, she knew I had a garment in the show, so she decided to attend that Monday evening. I went to bed early that night because I was leaving early the next morning with a friend for Texas and the Houston Quilt Festival. At midnight the phone rang. It was my friend all excited about the Fairfield Fashion Show. She said the crowd loved my garment and that it was the finale garment. Little did I know, that in the Fairfield Fashion Show. that was the place to be.

Needless to say, I was so excited, I didn't get much sleep that night. I can't tell you how proud I was the following Thursday night to see "my baby" on the stage for the first time. I cried. I will be forever grateful to Donna Wilder and her staff for giving me that first opportunity, for opening so many doors for me.

I have to say from a professional point of view it's all been an unbelievable experience for me. I've stayed in so many homes and made life long friends along the way. Some I stay in casual contact; with other's we've become wonderful friends. I have worked with students from coast to coast and the greatest reward for me is when I see "the light go on" in their eyes. The hugs at the end of the day, the emails that last long beyond my visit? How can I be so blessed?

I could not do what I do without a great husband who has encouraged my growth and is willing to share my time with other people because he knows it makes me happy. He's learned to take care of himself while I'm away. How lucky I am, that he's this way.

The hardest, but greatest job I've had is that of being a mother. The emotions we endure because we love our children. My children are the best in the world and I am so proud of them.

Our son Jeff was married July 26, 2003. He is a graduate of Denver Seminary and is on staff with the Navigators, a Christian ministry. His wife, Julie, is a wonderful addition to our family. The more I know Julie, the attribute I love the most about her, is her desire to be a part of our family. She is a strong Christian woman, a perfect help mate for our son. They both have a strong heart for missions and hope to serve in Ethiopia for a period of time in the future.

Our daughter Mary Karol is married to Craig McGee. She graduated from college with a math degree and has her Masters Degree in Education. She teaches at a community college in Omaha and works for the Omaha Public Schools in staff development. They now have a daughter Maddie and two great dogs. I lovingly call them my "grand dogs". Craig is an elementary principal and has his Masters Degree. He is the kind of man every mother wants for her daughter. He's the best. He's not my son-in-law, that's too impersonal, he's my son.

Our youngest is Sara, and of all our children, her heart is the biggest. She loves animals, and music has always been second nature to her. Her goal was to work with handicap children and dolphin therapy. Because of poor decisions, those dreams never came true. In the fall of 2002, I received the phone call parents never want to receive. She was in tears and it wasn't long before I was in tears, Sara was single and pregnant. I was absolutely crushed and emotionally torn apart. It was two months before I could tell my friends, it was just too hard to even say. I battled so hard over how to address this situation. I needed answers and they weren't coming. My new friend Patricia's idea helped me to deal with my sorrow.

In May of 2002, Patricia Louquet was my hostess at the Somer's, NY Quilt Show. At the time she had two grandchildren and I was only dreaming about my first grandbaby. Our discussion turned to baby quilts and she told me that she made a baby quilt to give the couples when they announced that a baby was on the way. This idea really gripped my heart, what a great way to celebrate a coming birth. That's what I wanted to do, celebrate new life from the very beginning. I started dreaming about the quilt I would make, when our only married children, Mary Karol and Craig finally announced a coming baby. I was excited about this project.

When Sara told us about her baby, I already had the pictures scanned for Mary Karol and Craig's quilt. My plan was to include pictures of the two of them as children. My dilemma was how did I make a quilt for Sara, what pictures could I use, with no daddy involved.

Soon after, Jeff was here and we had lunch. I still cried most of the time. Jeff's suggestion was to include pictures of all our family, grand parents and the many animals she loved over the years. What a great idea, this excited me and "A New Star on our Family Tree" was designed and made. This quilt was how I announced the baby to my group of friends. I had everyone over for breakfast right before Christmas and said I had something to show them, I finally had to say the "words", and it only got easier from there. Thank you Patricia for this wonderful idea, another way to love my kids.

A friend from church showed me the answer by her example. Her 17 year old granddaughter, Abbie, had a baby. Jenelle's example taught me that my only job was to love Sara and her baby. This is what God had called me to do since the day we brought her home from North Platte.

MaKayla Dawn Raymond was born six weeks early on May 9, 2003. She weighted 5 lbs and was in the neonatal ICU for 11 days. She has the sweetest little kisses and the biggest blue eyes. I waited a long time to be a "granny" and it was worth the wait.

Sara is doing a great job as a single Mom, I'm so proud of her. It's hard, but her main concern in life is that little girl.

Our second granddaughter Maddie McGee was born April 7, 2004. A little doll with big eyes. She weight 6 lbs. 12 oz. Another little girl to love.

As I said before, I don't remember a time when I didn't want to sew. Mother was the person who patiently taught her eager little daughter to use a needle and thread to sew doll clothes. Mom has Alzheimer's and doesn't remember those years, but she still knows all of us, for that I am grateful.

My sister, Karol Blakey, lives in Waco and cares for Mom. We talk almost every day, we have a way of motivating each other long distance.

Linda Goad is my Gothenburg "Sissie". She doesn't sew, but has encouraged me every step of the way. Everyone should have a Linda in their life.

My guardian angel friend is Brenda Kincaid from Danbury, NE. Brenda deals with severe health problems but is always ready to come when I need help. She is a great woman. I don't know what I would do without her.

Kay Figart's was my hostess in March 2001 in Conroe, TX. She's my "tiny" little friend who packs one of the strongest spirits I know. She has an understanding of what is right that is amazing and her gift of hospitality is the best!

Dorothy Williams of Florida is my sweet southern belle friend. We met at the AQS Wearable Contest in 2001 and been great friends ever since.

Sherrill Pryor of Ann Arbor MI, was my hostess in March 2002 in Ann Arbor, MI. She has her PHD in Ed. and is a professor at Grand Valley State University in MI. Her encouragement was what motivated me to "step up" and finally write this book.

My life has been the best. I have a wonderful husband and children and more friends than I can count who love me like family.

From coast to coast and around the world, there's another big family. One where all the members have a common bond. We share a wonderful connection, a common denominator, we're all "Sisters and Brothers of the Cloth."

I am where I am today because of all these people. Many have loved and encouraged me. I ask that you do the same for others. You know who I'm writing about; the young 4-H member who enters her first project in the fair; the guild friend who wants to enter a local show but feels her work is not worthy. Encourage then! If a ribbon is won, it just might be the start of something big.

For pictorial updates on the Raymond family to go my web site: Jenny's Family and Friends.

Introduction...........................

Remember.........Everything is a Process

Through all the years of my sewing for the public, I knew I had to make the most of my sewing time. I learned to be very methodical in my work. All supplies were lined up: the fabric prepared, pattern, interfacing, and notions. My machine was cleaned and a new needle, the correct size for my fabric type was inserted. Several bobbins were wound to help save time later. There was distilled water for my steam iron. All adjustments to patterns were made, then I cut the fabric and marked important information. Next I went to my serger to finish all seam edges. Then I machine stitched all seams that could be sewn together at that point. The next stop was the ironing board where I pressed open the seams on my project.

The purpose of this book and is to help you walk through the process of making a wonderful garment. We will start at the beginning of the process by making sure, we have the best equipment we can afford and the tools we need to do our job. Next is a great work area, I will tell you about my studio and it's floor plan. What goes into a studio so the space is productive for you.

Next is fabric and pattern selection, information on manipulating patterns to become your own. Good ideas on what I loving call "Planned Scrap" projects. This is great information for use as a quilter but also a great look for wearables. A "Planned Scrap" project gives an awesome display for fabric design and color. For me, the more fabrics the better. Also included is information on how to make a jacket using a sweatshirt foundation. Many design ideas for vest and jackets, illustrations so you can copy my ideas or take the idea and do something better with it. Loads of information on embellishments with lots of visuals. Next, are the finishing techniques, closures and even hand made buttons. Tips on lining and of course a label for your garment.

A good example of a process happened in 2002, when I designed "Diamonds are a Girl's Best Friend". I thought that the design would go together rather quickly. Oh boy, was I wrong! As it turned out; it took more time to make "Diamonds" than any other Fairfield or Bernina ensemble. I discovered that each process or step required to create "Diamonds" built on another. I had to be patient and couldn't rush ahead. By always approaching my work with the thought that each process must be accomplished to my very best ability, the end result will be my very best work.

In the spring of 2003, I had the opportunity to share with a lovely woman in Missouri about entering wearable shows. Her name is Joan Hanson and she won third place in the amateur division in Paducah that spring. Joan and I corresponded by email during that year and in this particular email she was focusing on being juried in again the next year. She was also interested in how to apply for the Bernina Fashion Show. This was my response to her, I think maybe it might help someone else.

" take each show one step at a time. You'll do just fine, just "step up" a little higher with your next garment since you're moving into the professional division. Keep in mind, the best part of creating another wonderful garment is, using new fabrics and ideas, the prize is just frosting on the cake.

The coat I had with me in Springfield, "Sunrise, Sunset" was entered in several shows and never won a thing. I still love it and was able to express myself using that particular collection of fabrics and ideas, so it was ok that I never won a prize.

Winning is simply a judges opinion that day, sometimes you win and sometimes you loose. If we win, we "fly with the geese" and it's humbling when we don't place. I've learned to take it all in stride. Start working towards a portfolio for the Bernina Show, if you make it, you've won the "biggest prize of all".

Are you ready to starting working on your portfolio?

I hope "Creative Techniques for Wearable" will assist you on that journey and help you to "step up".

General Information . . . .

So you want to be a quilter or seamstress? The first and foremost piece of equipment you will purchase is a sewing machine. If you have a good machine that performs as it should each time you sew, you'll love your new hobby. If your machine is of poor quality and reliability, you will soon loose interest, mainly because it is just too much work trying to make your sewing machine behave. The following is my advise on buying a machine.

Sewing Machines. . . . .

The first step in purchasing a sewing machine is finding a reputable machine dealer. That is not always an easy task. THEY ARE NOT ALL THE SAME. Ask for references if the dealer is a stranger to you. You may be offered a seemingly great deal, but in the long run, you pay for poor equipment.

Many years ago I was lulled into buying a machine that was part of an over-purchase of school machines. This machine was lauded as doing just about anything I needed it to do. I took the bait because I needed another machine for my store. and did not have a lot of money to spend. What a big waste of money! My help and I struggled through several years of sewing on that machine. To tell the truth, I am not sure what happened to it. I hope it is in a landfill somewhere, because that is where it belongs.

If it sounds like it's "too good a deal….. a great price, only $299.00"…..it might be a good idea to run as fast as you can to your nearest dealer that sells only name brand machines.

For your sake, make an informed decision so that you can enjoy your machine for many years to come.

Quality is Important

If you are serious about sewing, a quality sewing machine is an absolute must. Quality sewing machines are not cheap, but are a great investment. A quality machine means you will have few repairs and little down time, and will be ready to sew when you are ready to sew. If your budget is tight, I suggest a reconditioned name-brand machine.

Not all Machines are Created Equally

In the 40 years I've been married, I've had 4 different brand machines. I made the decision in the mid 90"s to spend my money on the "BMW" of sewing machines, the Bernina. I will never purchase another brand of sewing machine. In overall performance they can not be beat. I've watched students struggle with their machines; few brands seem to handle as precisely as the Bernina. There are other quality machines on the market, but I am biased. I recently taught at a national conference and my opinions still stand strong. For your information I do not receive a free machine from Bernina, except for the 135 which I won. I've paid for all of my machines.

My primary machine is the Bernina Artista 180. I also use the Activa 135, as well as my very first Bernina, the 930. Recently I was told that the 930 is worth more today than what I paid for it in 1984. If you are familiar with the Singer Featherweight made early in the 20th century, you will understand why I consider the 930 the "featherweight" of the 90's!

"BERNINA® 930 Sewing Machine",

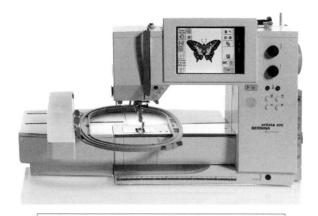

"The BERNINA® *Artista* 200E Sewing Machine with Embroidery System".

Visit
www.berninausa.com
for more product information, creative
projects and sewing tips

Sewing Machine Add-on

Machine Flatbed Extender:

These are wonderful additions to your free standing sewing machine as they add a much larger flatbed area. They measure approximately 18"x 24" and are available from your machine dealer or can be ordered from your favorite fabric/notions store. For me it's a must!

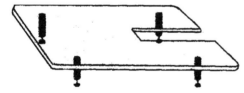

Machine Needles
Premium machine needles are a must for quality machine stitching.

If you have trouble with your machine's stitch quality, try switching to a **Schmetz** needle. Schmetz universal needles vary in size from 8 to 19. The 19's are huge and great for heavy projects. The Schmetz jeans needles range in size from 10 to 16 and are also available in a double needle. Schmetz also makes stretch, twin stretch, ball point, leather, hemstitch, self threading, triple, topstitch, embroidery, double embroidery, quilting and twin needles that range from 2.5 to 6.0.

Remember to change your machine needle often. New needles feel extremely sharp, and after approximately 5-8 hours of sewing they should be replaced. The type of fabric being sewn will make a difference. For example, needles dull very quickly with silk. If your machine sounds like a tractor, it could be you have not changed the needle for a long time! A dull needle makes for a noisy sewing machine and poor stitch quality.

Are you having trouble with thread snags? Try a new needle!

The eye of a needle is punched-out during the manufacturing process and it is difficult to make the eye smooth. In fact, only thirty percent of manufactured needles pass inspection and the other seventy percent are melted down to start over. When you open a new packet of needles, approximately ten percent of those new needles have burs that may snag the thread. If you have a problem with a particular thread, even if it is new, try a new needle. This often solves the problem. If it does not solve the problem, you might consider changing the spool of thread, as it might be faulty.

Spare Machine Parts?
"I need a new felt pad for my machine!"

I recall a lady who went into a machine repair shop and wanted to replace the felt pad in her machine. In reality, the lint in the machine feed dogs and the bobbin hook area had built up for so long, was so heavy, that she thought it was supposed to be there! The repairman kindly informed the lady that there was no need to replace the felt pad. Instead, the repairman advised the lady to clean her machine feeddogs and the bobbin hook area when she changed her needle. Once she put this into practice, she noticed a positive change in her stitch. The moral of the story is to keep those feeddogs clean!

To clean the bobbin hook area, remove the bobbin hook and use a small piece of cloth to wipe this area clean. My little cloth is usually covered with grime. I place one drop of oil on my bobbin hook and replace it in my machine. If I do not follow the above steps, I **hear** the difference in my sewing machine. Check the Owner's Manual for your machine for tips on how to properly clean your machine.

Creating a Great Workspace ....my little bit of Heaven.

My wish for every seamstress is a place to call their own. I have been so fortunate, because for 30 years I have had just such a place. In our former home, it was a small room that was once a kitchen. In our home today it is a wonderful 28'x 15' studio, that's just the way I want it. For my work, this room is very important and I am so grateful.

For 20 years my studio was a 16' x16' room that was built for my use. Over time, I filled it up with storage units, a desk etc. and could hardly move, and I had no room for a design wall.

Because we have a lake home not far from Gothenburg, our children always stay out there when they come home. We had three extra bedrooms upstairs, as well as my studio. I decided to "take back" two of the bedrooms to use as my studio. The wall was taken out between the two rooms (illustrated by broken lines on the floor plan, next page) and the result was a great work area, approximately 28'x 15'.

Now I have a sewing area, design wall and a corner for my office, which was located in the basement. There are three closets, and a built-in chest of four deep drawers. I moved storage units from the old studio and several pieces of furniture. In one of the original bedrooms was a built in desk and book case, they were moved to different locations within the studio. The only thing that had to be built was the top of my cutting table. A retired shop school teacher did the work. His charges were reasonable and his work was wonderful. I did the painting, staining and wallpaper to save on cost.

Soon I hope to replace the double window by my machine table. The bottom edge of the present window is at eye level when I am sitting at my machine. I want to lower the edge the top of the table; so I can see our yard full of trees, and beautiful birds, when I am sewing.

The first night it was finished, and all cleaned up, I walked around and felt like a princess in a castle. When I was six years old, the girl across the street had a play house. I always wanted a playhouse of my own (that would be so cool) but it never happened.

Now I have my own "play room" and it's the best. It's wonderful to have a space all my own. I feel so very blessed. When we're old and the house sells some day, I'll let future generations decide the room's fate. Hopefully a quilter will buy this house and her dreams can come true as mine have.

True Confession time..............Oink, Oink, Oink, Oink

When I work on a project, I'm a "pig." My "play room" is a mess! My studio is seldom picked up, but that's ok, it's my little bit of heaven. I just close the door and no body but me has to see my "piles", unless Bob peeks his head in the door. I mean well and fully intend to pick up and put away, that will probably happen when pigs fly.

Comfort while sewing

Did you know that if you lower your chair when sewing, so that you are looking at and not down to your machine, you can eliminate most of your upper back and neck pain. A chiropractor gave me this advise many years ago, after going in for monthly treatments. I took his advise and it was a year before I needed another adjustment. Now, I use a chair that can be raised and lowered and gives good lower back support. One problem with inexpensive chairs is that they are hard to adjust to an upright position, they tend to lean backwards, this is hard on my back.

Before purchasing a chair, check the following:
* Is the seat comfortable? too hard, too soft?
* Will the adjustments "hold" for the back of the chair?
* Adjustment for chair height?

Floor plan for my studio ....

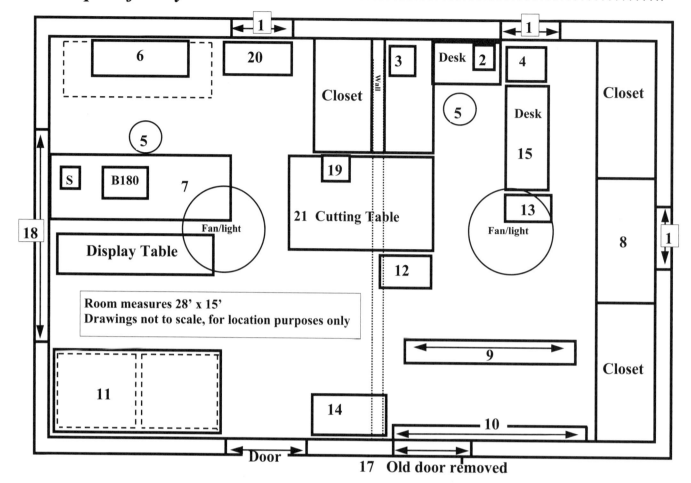

Room measures 28' x 15'
Drawings not to scale, for location purposes only

17 Old door removed

1. Windows
2. Printer
3. Computer monitor on corner desk unit.
4. Scanner
5. Swivel desk chair
6. Book case recycled from original bedroom, with design table below
7. Machine table from my old studio, measures 26"x 68". Two drawer units on each end.
   My Bernina 180 & (S) serger sit on this unit.
8. Built in Chest of drawers (4)
9. Track lighting - shines on Design Wall
10. Design Wall - 8'x11' Core foam/Felt page 12.
11. Upper storage unit from old studio
    H 63"x W 56" x D 26. Below this unit are two old pattern cabinets from my fabric store.
12. Small portable island made for the kitchen, but works wonderfully in my studio
13. Low storage chest
14. Antique walnut chest of drawers-storage for gift wrap paper, bags, ribbons, small gifts.

15. This desk was original in the bedroom on the left. Originally it was built in with book shelf (6) over this desk.
16. These lines represent the wall that was removed between the two rooms.
17. This was the original location of the door into the right bedroom. The door was removed and finished with dry wall. Removing this door, gave me a large area for my design wall.
18. Large window by my machine table. It sits 1 1/2 feet above my top edge of my machine table. I plan to put a large window in here that will start at the top edge of my machine table. Our back yard is full of trees and I want to watch the birds while I sew.
19. Small TV mounted on wall stand.
20. Bernette steam press sitting on baker's rack. I recently purchased this from a friend for $35.00. I'm sorry I didn't buy one years ago.
21. Cutting table moved from old studio, measures 4'x6' shelving with doors underneath.

Setting up a Cutting Table

A very important part of your studio is a good cutting table. It should be at a height that enables you to stand straight, eliminating the need to bend over your work. Bending makes for a very sore back at the end of the day.

My cutting table is the perfect height for me. It measures 72" x 40". There is a large storage area underneath with shelves. The small wall in back of my cutting table has four electrical outlets, and I recently purchased a power strip to increase the number of outlets. On the same wall, up and out of the way is a small TV on a swivel wall shelf. I can watch television without taking up table space.

Most sewers and quilters do not have a large area to themselves, especially if they still have children at home. Before remodeling, my solution was a large antique pool table in our basement; it made a perfect cutting table. A 6' or 8' banquet table with a full sheet of plywood (4'x8') placed on top, makes a great portable cutting table. Plywood is rough, so cover with a vinyl table cloth. If the board is used only for cutting, wrap the edges of the vinyl cloth around to the back side and secure with heavy tacks. Another use for these boards is to expand table seating when you have guests for dinner.

For cutting ease I purchased a extra large, 40"x 72" cutting mat marked with a grid for my pool table. It now sits on the cutting table in my studio. This mat works well for cutting fashion fabrics as pins can be stuck into the mat to hold fabric in place.

These mats are available in 13 different sizes; from 5"x7" to 60"x120". If you cannot find these mats at your local sewing center, write, e-mail or call for pricing. I can order one from my distributor, and have it shipped to your front door.

Check www.jennyraymond.com for contact information.

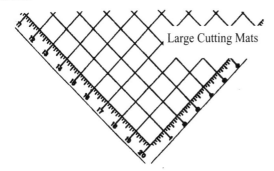
Large Cutting Mats

Cutting Fashion Fabric

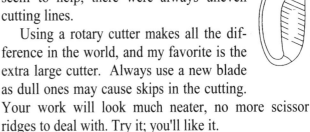

For the many years I made bridal garments, I battled slippery fabrics. Even with the greatest care, they wiggled and squirmed. Using sharp scissors did not seem to help, there were always uneven cutting lines.

Using a rotary cutter makes all the difference in the world, and my favorite is the extra large cutter. Always use a new blade as dull ones may cause skips in the cutting. Your work will look much neater, no more scissor ridges to deal with. Try it; you'll like it.

Good Lighting is a Must

Whether in your design area or at the sewing machine, good lighting is an absolute must. I have a halogen swan neck lamp that sits to the right of my machine. I crook it so that it shines right on my sewing project. Lights with magnifiers are available, even portable ones that can be taken when you leave home. It's sad but true, the older we get, the more important is good light.

The design wall needs good light. When I remodeled my studio, I installed track lighting. It really made a difference. Before everything was in shadows, even with good room light fixtures.

Building a Design Wall

I do all my design work on a design wall. In my studio it measures 8'x 11'. It is made from core foam, a product found at a home improvement store, covered with neutral colored felt, that will not interfere with the color schemes of my projects.

Thumb tack   Felt to cover wall

Benefits of a Design Wall

The benefit of using a design wall is that you can view your project from a distance. When displayed in a show, quilts are viewed at a distance, not up close. I not only put my quilt projects on the design wall, but all wearable projects are placed there as well. I cannot imagine trying to do it any other way! Years ago I would lay everything out on the floor, then climb up on a table or chair so that I could look down on my work. That was back in the "olden days".

Since then, I have learned that using a design wall gives me a better perspective. Find a wall that you can claim as your own, it will make a world of difference in your work. For a time, the only large wall near my studio was one in a hall. To view the wall at a distance, I had to step back into a bedroom. It was better than nothing at all. I admit I was lucky my husband never complained about the felt I attached to the wall with thumb tacks. "Thank you Bob".

Table Easel Design Wall

When designing quilt blocks, I use a table easel with a cushioned press/design board. Press boards are available from a number of companies. They are covered with heavy fabric, marked with a 1-inch grid and are padded. Place a small piece of felt on this board and you have a design board that you can place near your sewing machine. Mine is placed on the design table behind my machine.

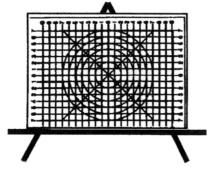

Another use for Cushioned Press Board

When I am working on a large quilt project that's displayed on my large design wall and I have the project ready to sew, there can be a problem taking all the small pieces of fabric to the machine. I find that the press board comes in handy. Take a small section from the design wall and lay on the press board in the order they were on the wall. Now you can take that part of your project to the machine for sewing.

Wall hanging Projects

Use a flannel back vinyl tablecloth for small projects.

Dress Form & Mannequin

Several years ago I purchased a Dritz dress form. What a valuable tool it has been for me as a wearable designer. Not only do I use it to fit garments, but also for placing embellishments on my garments. For example, when I was making "Arabesque", I wanted to embellish this garment with silk ribbon roses and flowers of all sizes. By placing the dress on the dress form and then adding the flowers to the dress, I could see how they would look when the dress was on a person. I did the same with the coat as the shoulder area of the cape was covered in large silk roses. By hanging the cape on the dress form, I could place the roses in the exact place.

Recently I discovered another use for my dress form, I turned it into a mannequin.

For years I struggled with taking photos of my work. During the process of writing this book, I ordered a flex body mannequin from a source in New York. Some how my order was lost in the cracks and it was late in coming. I tried borrowing, but that was not real successful. The only thing I could find was one of wicker style, that had a real posture problem. This is how I transformed my dress form into a decent mannequin. I took a black turtleneck and cut a circle of black fabric, then sewed the circle to close off the turtle neck. I slipped the turtleneck shirt onto the dress form, then a long black skirt. I feel it served me well. I wish it had arms as the flex body does, but it worked in a pinch to photo garments for this book. I do look forward to having the reasonably priced flex body for future use.

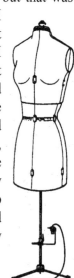

My Favorite Notions . . . . . . **These notions are an absolute must in my sewing room!**

The small notions we use with our sewing projects make our work so much easier.
There are so many little gems. Good sewing tools are very important in the sewing process.

Magnetic Pin Cushion

It quickly picks up pins that are on the floor, which is where most of mine seem to be. I can not imagine not having at least one in my studio.

Sewing Pins that are Extra long, sharp, with round heads

I love these pins because they are so easy to handle and pick up. Using them, I get a good bite of the fabric I am working on, and because of the round head, they are easily retrieved from my carpet. When purchasing these pins, be sure the package is marked sharp.

Scissors

Anyone who works with cloth must have a good pair of scissors. From the many years of selling notions and being a seamstress, I think it's hard to beat *Gingher* scissors. They are very sharp and, with care, stay that way for a long time. *Gingher* has over thirty different kinds of scissors from which to choose. I have four different *Gingher* scissors, they are expensive but worth the money. You won't believe the difference.

One day during the years I had my store, I received a call from a customer in Hershey, NE. She was in the market for a pair of 8" bent trimmers. Gothenburg is an hour from Hershey and she wanted them in a hurry. I had a pair on hand and she asked me to call our airport to see if they had a car her husband could use. He was going to fly to Gothenburg in their small plane to pick up these scissors! In short, the airport had a car for her husband and Marilyn got her new pair of *Ginghers*. Once you have used them, you will go to any limits for another pair!

Ailene's Jewell It

This is a great glue product. It is washable when used on fabric. As a precaution, be sure to check the label for proper use. When first applied, it is cloudy, but will dry clear. See page 96.

Fray Check

What would I do without Fray Check to keep the edges of fabric from raveling, ribbons from fraying, clipped threads from coming loose and many other uses. A whole bottle of Fray Check was used when machine quilting my second Fairfield Ensemble, "Joseph's Jubilation." Because the design started and stopped in the middle of the ensemble, the stitching started and stopped what seemed to be a thousand times. I was afraid the metallic thread would come out where back-stitched. I applied a small drop of Fray Check and my worries were over! To apply tiny little drops, dip a pin tip into the solution and then touch the spot to be sealed.

Bobbinsaver

This is a blue plastic ring that holds over 20 bobbins. This is an absolute must in my sewing studio. It actually keeps my bobbins nice and tidy, something that's never happened in the past. It could be the best $6.00 you'll ever spend.

Liquid Silicon

This product prevents your machine from skipping stitches. My favorite brand is **Sewer's Aid**. When a small drop is placed at the top of your machine needle, it will keep sticky residue from gumming up your sewing machine needle. Repeat as needed. Sewer's Aid is also great when stitching with metallic and rayon threads. Spread three rows of liquid across the spool and let it soak into the thread. Place a small drop at the top of your machine needle as well. When hand sewing, apply Sewer's Aid to your hand needle for easier penetration of the fabric. Sewer's Aid is also the answer for sewing over non-roll elastic. The needle will slide right through instead of popping up and not sewing properly.

Have you tried a **Ballpoint Bodkin** used for lace and elastic insertion, turning bias tubing, and inserting cable cord into bias tubing. .The bodkin is about 7" long with an needle eye for threading if needed and a ball on the other end for easy penetration of lace, casing or bias tube. I must share my favorite use for this little tool.

1. Cut and stitch a length of bias tubing.
2. To turn tubing, insert bodkin into tube, ball first. Bring the needle eye right to one end. Use a needle and thread to tack bodkin to one side of tube. Secure. Push ball end of bodkin through to the other end. The tube is turned.

3. This is the fun part. Take a length of cable cord to be inserted into tubing. Run a needle and thread through the eye of the bodkin and into the end of cable cord. Wrap the thread tightly around the cable cord several times and secure. This is the trick! Take about three inches of scotch tape. Start a little past the bodkin eye and wrap the tape around the cord proceeding up the bodkin until you've enclosed the threads of the cord in the tape. Use your fingers to roll the tape so it flattens out. Do you see what can be accomplished now? Insert the ball of the bodkin into one end of the bias tube, pull and work the taped section up into the tube, then pull through to the other end. Turn to pages 115-118 for ideas on using the cord filled tubing. Ordering information is on page 126.

Did you know?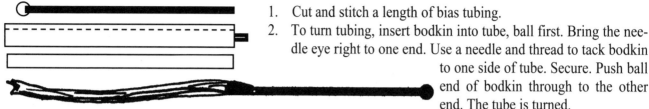

- You can cut off a polyester zipper if you don't have the correct length. Simply tack across the zipper at the desired length, and cut 1/2" below tack. This can't be done with a metal zipper.

- Small rotary cutters are dandy for cutting out blocks using templates. I like using the small one because it is so much easier to control in tight areas.

- If you need extra-wide, heavy elastic, stretch-belting works well as a substitute. It works especially well when you need elastic for the bottom of a jacket.

Irons Better Safe than Sorry!

Many years ago, I left the house, forgetting to unplug my iron. After *several days* I came home to find that it had turned over on the ironing board, leaving a huge black mark. It is a miracle our home did not burn down! The moral of the story? Always purchase irons with an automatic turn-off function. Despite having to restart my iron frequently, it is worth the effort for safety's sake.

How much time??????

People often ask me how much time it takes to make my ensembles. I keep a note card by my machine and use it to keep track of the time I spent on a project. Keep a record of this information in a small notebook, that way if someone asks you to make a particular garment for them, you'll have a good idea of the time you spent and what you need to charge. I once designed a vest for a lady thinking $300.00 would cover my time and materials with ease. I was wrong! Another lesson learned in life. If you are going to sell your garments or quilts, it is very important that you are properly compensated for your efforts and talents.

Besides, it would be fun to look back several years later and read the history of your sewing.

Resource Information........................

Quilter's Insurance

Several years ago, to my surprise, I discovered that my homeowners insurance does not cover my Wearables or quilts while away from home. If you desire this type of insurance coverage on your quilts while you are away from home, contact Chris Johnson, in Phoenix, AZ. Her phone number is 602-395-91. Tell her you are interested in a policy through the Society of Quilters, a special policy they carry that will cover this situation. It's through Hartford Insurance Company.

Quilt & Wearable Appraisals

Marcia Kaylakie, AQS Certified Appraiser
3703 Turkey Creek Drive
Austin, TX 78730
(512) 502-0383
marciark@earthlink.net
www.texasquiltappraiser.com

She does all types of appraisals for quilts (antique, vintage, and modern), art quilts, wearable art and garments, liturgical vestments and pediments.

Marcia worked for me for the first time in January of 2003 and I was very happy with her work.

Fabric Resources

Silk Dupioni Resource

Leo Moses Silks & Interiors 214-744-7455
Web sight under construction email
lmsilks@sbcglobal.net
121 colors 44" silk Dupioni available
75 colors 54" silk Dupioni available
Elegant silk drapes made to order
Leo Moses Textiles wholesale 214-654-0156
email leomoses@sbcglobal.net
Mountain fleece solids and prints/24 solid and 60 prints available.

Exotic Silks—offers both retail and wholesale fabrics.
http://www.exoticsilks.com/index.html

Kaplan Fabrics—this is a great retail source. They are very good about sending samples.
866-531-4819 (Toll free)
(816) 531- 4818
438 Ward Parkway
Kansas City, Missouri 64112

Denver Fabrics
303-730-2777
2777 W. Belleview
Between Santa Fe & Federal
M-F 10-8 Sat 10-6 Sun 12-5
http://www.denverfabrics.com
Web Site Customers: 1-866-996-4573

Glorious Fabrics
http://www.gloriousfabrics.com/cgi-bin/store/
commerce.cgi?&cart_id=3663991.15868

Cherrywood Fabrics-Featuring Suede Look Cottons
888-298-0967
http://www.cherrywoodfabrics.com
They can usually be reached by phone M-F between 9 a.m. and 4 p.m. CST. If they are not available, you can leave a message on their answering machine.

Fashion Fabric Club
http://www.fashionfabricsclub.com/home

E-Quilter-"Your Fabric Store for Quilting, Sewing & Fashion"
877-FABRIC-3 (Toll free)
303-527-0856
Fax: 303-527-0042
http://www.equilter.com

St. Theresa Textiles
http://www.sttheresatextile.com

Jane Sassaman Fabrics
http://www.janesassaman.com/index.html
(Click on "Online Store")

Butterick/McCall's/Vogue Patterns
http://www.butterick.com/index.html
Please note: I've noticed the very newest patterns are not listed on the web site. My guess, this is to give retail merchants the opportunity to sell the pattern before the major companies list them on their web sites.

Park Bench Patterns
619-269-9808
Fax: 619-269-9809
PO Box 191399
San Diego, CA 92159-1399
http://www.parkbenchpatterns.com

Rama Buttons
Tia Montague
2411 Lincoln Ave. SE   Olympia WA 98501
360-786-8851   elensul@hotmail.com
See "Quilting Arts" Magazine Spring 2002 for article.

Full and Sassy Patterns
http://www.fullfab.com/purrfection

Speed Stitch
http://www.speedstitch.com

Cheaptrims.com
http://www.cheeptrims.com/default.asp

Sewing Machine Manuals
http://pages.sewing-machine-manuals.com

Fabrics.net
http://www.fabrics.net
To find a specific type of fabric you can go to
http://www.fabrics.net/swatch

Fashion Designing-this site has the work of many well
known designers in the fashion industry. It is a good
place to get ideas.
http://www.atelierdesigners.com

Notes. . . . .

Patterns..............so many from which to choose!

Selecting Your Patterns

As makers of wearables, we should take full advantage of the great assortment of patterns that are available on  the retail market. A number of patterns are available today with great ethnic design and style. I purchase them because all the work has been done for me. I can make the pattern my own by modifying it if I chose to and by using my own assortment of fabrics and trims. I utilize pattern tracing fabric or paper, magic markers, quilt rulers, scotch tape and whatever other tools I might need.

The four largest pattern companies, Butterick, McCalls, Simplicity, and Vogue have great patterns. Many work well for wearable art. In addition, a number of talented designers have published their patterns. Some are Lois and Diane Erickson, June Colburn, and Judy Murrah and Barbara Weiland. Murrah and Weiland have produced a wonderful jacket pattern I like called "Plain & Fancy". Also look for patterns from Park Bench Pattern, Purrfection and so many others.

There can be problems with the sizing information on patterns produced by the smaller companies; it is not always consistent. I suggest that you always make a muslin for these patterns. It is worth the extra effort because of their wonderful style and design.

Organizing Your Patterns

I consider myself to being a fairly creative person but not a very patient one. I have never liked trying to place all the pattern tissues back into one of the small envelopes. In fact, I like  *Stretch and Sew* patterns because they come in large envelopes! When I purchase other brands of patterns, I place them in gallon-size (or larger) zip-lock bags. Then everything is together when it is needed the next time!

Which Pattern Did I Use????

I sometimes forget which pattern I used for a project. I have a few strategies that help me remember. One strategy includes tapping a small swatch of the fabric that was used to the outside of the pattern.

A second idea is to place a fabric swatch and the pattern number on a note card or the back of a picture of the project. Then save these in a small picture-album book. This is handy because it can include any notes about the project.

Tracing Your Patterns

I suggest that you trace your pattern onto tracing paper or fabric especially if it is one you will be using again. This way you can draw any pattern modifications on the paper or design areas.

Pattern Sizing................never assume the pattern is going to fit

For the 30+ years I sewed for the public, I was given the opportunity to fit every body size and shape imaginable. Most of the time, it was difficult and took some serious thought and imagination. With no formal training in textile design and fitting, I learned this "by the seat of my pants" along with all other sewing skills that I developed over the years. Following are some of the skills I learned, very important details in the process of wearable sewing.

Make a Muslin

For a good fit on most patterns, I suggest making a muslin. Muslin is an inexpensive, utility type fabric, with many uses and is excellent for pattern fitting. The term to "make a muslin" refers to cutting your pattern sections out of muslin or like fabric, transferring all pattern notations and markings, then pinning seam allowances together for fitting purposes. After getting a correct fit, use the muslin as your pattern, not the original tissue.

Pattern Size

Basic rule: fit all garments that are being made! Patterns may be common in sizing, but most of us are not common in build.

It is very important to know and use your correct pattern size.

You can't lie to a pattern and that's the truth!

Pattern catalogues from companies such as McCalls, Simplicity, Butterick or Vogue provide complete information on how to measure your body.

My experience with patterns being published today by the "Big 4" pattern companies is that the patterns are styled with a close fit. When people mature, their overall body size increases even if they do not gain a lot of weight. Much of this extra size is noticed in in the arms, shoulders, chest and waist on a woman. All of this must be taken into consideration when you purchase a pattern.

A person's body build has everything to do with the adjustments that need to be made on patterns. My daughter Sara is tall; and although she has a short waist length, her legs are long. Because patterns are drafted for a close fit, I have to make changes or the garment will not fit.

A. Bust and Hips

The measurements on pattern sheets for bust and hips are exact as listed on the pattern. You need at least 2 to 4 inches of ease or your garment will not fit. In other words, if your exact hip measurement is 36", you will need another 2 to 4 inches added to the pattern for ease, as illustrated on the skirt drawing. The amount of ease necessary is governed by the type of fabric being used. Knits take less ease, whereas heavier woven fabrics may take more. I suggest you make a muslin to be sure of a correct fit, then use the marked muslin as your pattern.

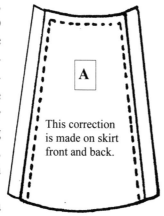

This correction is made on skirt front and back.

Measure 9" down from the waist, the distance from seam line to seam line on the front and back patterns. Add together the two numbers. For example we will say the measurement is 36". Now measure your hips across the fullest part. If your hips measure 38", you need to add two inches to the pattern, that's an addition 1/2" to each seam. Next we account for ease. Add the amount of ease needed for your fabric type. Divide the total ease by four, then add that amount to each side seam as well. The addition to each side seam includes, any addition needed because of your hip measurement and the amount needed for ease. Be sure and make a complete muslin of the skirt or pants to check for fit and adjustments that need to be made.

If you wear a size 10 in a ready made skirt, don't be surprised if in a straight skirt pattern, you need a size 12 or 14.

B. Bodice

Over time, my rule has been to add seam allowance to shoulder, side and back when cutting a muslin. Mark original seam lines on muslin with red magic marker.

You can always take in the additional seam allowance but it cannot be add on if it is too small. In this case, you would need to cut another muslin and start over!

Pin together at shoulder and side seams. After the muslin is on the person, pin baste the back seam, now fit. Mark new adjustment on the muslin in black magic marker.

Next trim away excess fabric and leave 5/8" seam allowance on the muslin. The muslin is ready for use as your pattern.

Check for these Adjustments

Back waist measurement

I am short, but have a long back waist measurement. Although I'm only 5'4", but I need a long torso swim suit. Make this adjustment on pattern if necessary. Have a friend measure from the round bone at the base of your skull to the small of your back.

C. Tight arm hole

This is an adjustment I make for my daughter, Sara. Split the bodice pattern as illustrated. If you split the bodice pattern, the same adjustment must be made on the sleeve as illustrated.

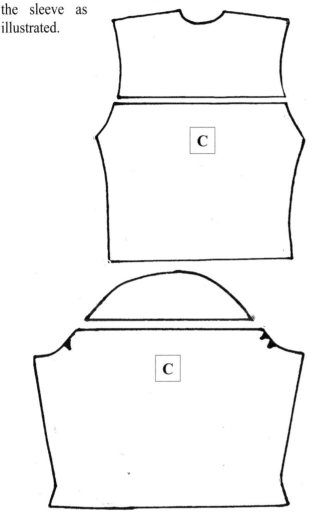

D. Shoulder Seam Addition

If you add to the shoulder seam and there is a sleeve, then you must add to the sleeve pattern as illustrated by the dotted line. Cut muslin of new sleeve to test for proper fit.

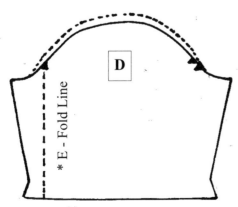

E. Gapping Arms Eye

Often women with a large bust line have a problem with a gapping arms eye. This is easily fixed by placing a dart as illustrated. Make a muslin of the sleeve pattern to see how it is going to fit after this adjustment. *You may need to take in the front sleeve section by folding out a little bit along the dotted line as illustrated at **(D)** by dotted lines. This adjustment can be made for bodice front on jackets, vests and dresses.

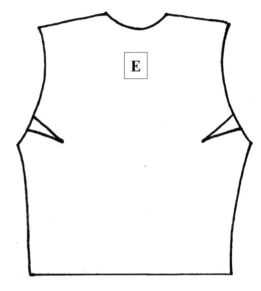

F. Sleeve Length

Most sleeve patterns are tapered to the wrist. Because of this the facing for the sleeve is shaped to fold back up the sleeve. All sleeve adjustments must be made above the facing line as illustrated. This adjustment is marked on most patterns. It is important that you know the correct sleeve length before you cut the fabric.

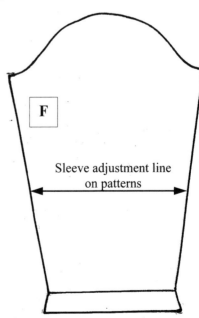

Sleeve adjustment line on patterns

Pattern Modification........................…...…making it my own

Taking a simple pattern and modifying it to create design areas is an important skill to learn when making wearables. I have been doing this for years and don't think twice about "doing my own thing" with printed patterns. I interchange sleeves and sleeve heads, lengthen or shorten jackets and widen or taper pant legs. Pattern can be divided into different sections, and then sew it back together again.

Pattern Modification for Jackets

If you plan on changing the length of a jacket, remember to adjust all corresponding facing pattern pieces as well.

The jacket below is a good example of using pattern modification. This pattern is an out-of-date *Stretch and Sew*, but a good example. The yoke on this jacket was designed as one piece, but I wanted to use many colors of silk, so I divided the yoke as described under Creative Yokes (next page) and designed an awesome jacket. Both the front and back yoke and lower portions of this jacket were changed.

The sketches in the next column are examples of pattern modification. Work with a 24" quilt ruler to divide the pattern into different sections. It is very important to remember where you draw a line and create a new section., seam allowance must be added at the drawn line for each new section. Be sure to mark the grain line on each new pattern section.

The following is a simple illustration.
A. Illustrates a bodice pattern.
B. Illustrates where a simple modification will be made.
C. Illustrates the two new sections cut apart and seam allowance added on the modification line.

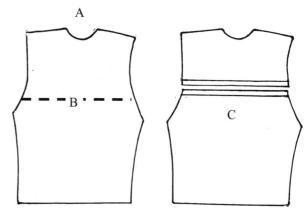

The following are examples of pattern modification.

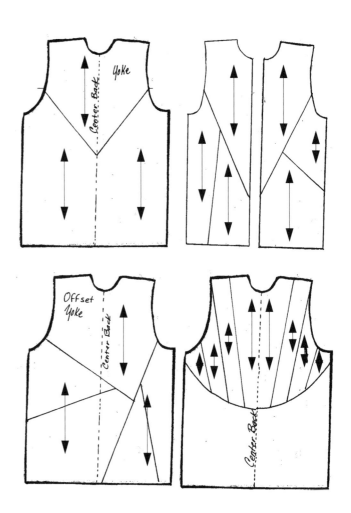

Creative Yokes

Patterns that have interesting shaped yokes can easily be turned into designer wearables. And guess who the designer is? You! Use the following illustration to create your own designer yoke. This same principal works on any garment section. Divide the yoke into sections as illustrated. Cut these sections apart. Next trace each section adding 1/4 seam allowance along sides marked with "x x x". Note grain line of pattern on each piece. Cut out each new section using fabrics that coordinate with your dress or blouse fabric (lames, cottons, satins, etc) then carefully sew them back together. Press well. If delicate fabrics are used, iron with a press cloth. After you assemble the yoke, use your imagination to machine quilt this area. Heavy quilting is not advisable as it shrinks the area quilted.

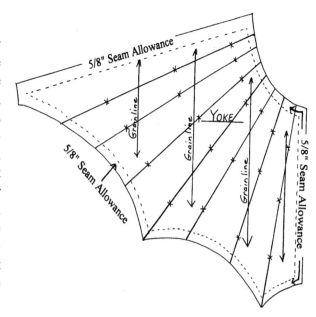

Sleeve Modification

Many patterns today have elastic on the cuff edge of the sleeve. At times they are drafted with an extremely wide cuff area. I don't like wide sleeves as I feel as though I have wings. To modify the cuff edge on a sleeve pattern, first determine the correct length for the sleeve. This can be accomplished by pinning fronts and back foundation pieces together. Next pin the sleeve on at the shoulder/sleeve seam. If shoulder pads are used, place one in at this point as it will affect your sleeve length. Pin desired sleeve length on sleeve foundation and add 2" for the hem. Now reduce the width of sleeve (see illustration). Use a 24" quilt ruler to find the center point on bottom of the sleeve. Measure out from there 5-6" on each side and mark this point. Draw a line from that point to upper sleeve seam (see illustration). Add a 5/8" seam allowance. Do not forget to adjust the sleeve facing. See bottom of page 19.

Optional Jacket Finish

Often when I make a jacket or vest that has a straight front finish at the bottom, it does not hang straight. The bottom of both sides tend to turn in or out. It can be frustrating!

To help eliminate this problem I often round off this edge. This is easily done, by using a plastic butter tub or ice cream container lid as a template. The same adjustment can be made for the upper lapel area as well, and partially opened side seams. If your jacket is cut out and not hanging the way you want, draw this new stitching line on the back side of your jacket section to make sure of exact placement. Stitch on the traced line and then cut away excess fabric. Once it's cut, it's cut!

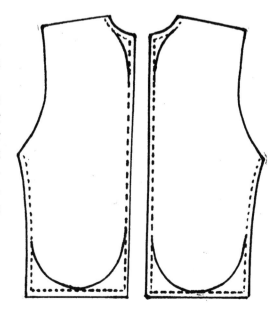

Pattern Modifications for Jacket or Shirt Right Front

It is fairly simple to modify the right front of a shirt or jacket pattern. Illustration **A** shows a pattern with a simple straight edge front opening.

Use pattern tracing material to do these types of modifications. Often it is helpful, to use a 24" quilt ruler and pencil to draw a grid on the tracing material. This helps to assure your design is being drawn straight and it gives you guide lines. This is what I did, when I drew the diamonds on the coat for "Diamonds are a Girl's Best Friend".

The following examples of modifications that can be made. The dotted section illustrates the position of the left side of the jacket, accounting for the area needed for buttonholes and buttons. As always, I suggest you make a muslin of your new drawing to assure a good fit.

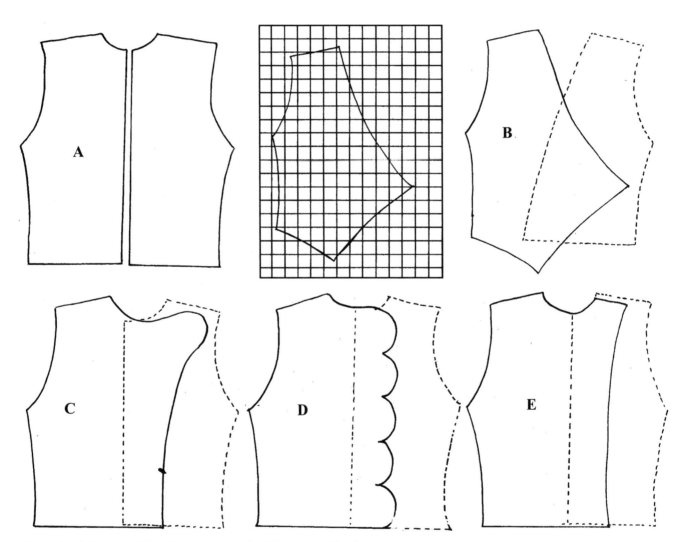

Several of these modifications are ones that I have used in the past.

C was used on "Diamonds are a Girl's Best Friend". See page 76.

E was used on "Starlight Rhapsody" my first Fairfield ensemble. See page 75.

To draft **D**, use the lid of a small butter container for the scallop edge.

Interface your extension well, to accommodate buttonholes and for good body.

> Never through away old patterns, save them for a garage sale or give them to a local charity the provides for the needs of others. Be sure all pieces are still in the pattern, most people have no idea how to draft new pattern pieces.

Vest Back Waist Adjustment

On most vest patterns, a tie is placed right below center back (see **A**). I don't like this design as it adds a flounce in the back and most women don't need a flounce over their rear area. I make a modification that works well.

First of all, mark center back on your vest. Assemble the vest as your pattern illustrates, sewing the top fabric and lining together at shoulder seams. Do not sew side seams together. Form a **casing** on the lower edge of the finished vest back, by marking a line that is 1 1/4" from the lower edge x 9"long, as illustrated at **B**. This is positioned over center back. Stitch along this marked line through the top and lining fabric. This will form a casing for the elastic. Insert a 6" piece of 1" wide non-roll elastic. Secure both ends of the elastic, stitching through the top fabric and lining.

Adding a casing to a ready made vest.

Mark and stitch as above. At the end of each stitching line, make a slit in the lining fabric. Insert elastic into the casing. Stitch the elastic at each end of the casing. Fold the raw edges of the slit under, bring the folded edges together and hand stitch in place.

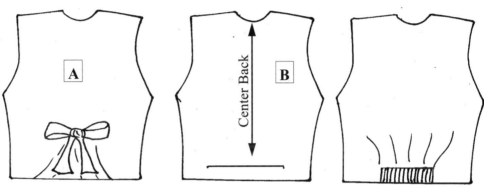

Foundation Fabric

I seldom use batting in my garment, unless I am making an ensemble for a show and it is required. The reason I do not use batting is it eliminates a heat factor. Instead, I use a foundation fabric. The foundation fabric can be fit and modifications made. It also gives the jacket fabric extra body for embellishing.

I bought that pink elephant fabric for what?

The foundation can be any piece of fabric. Muslin has been mentioned; but you can also use that really awful piece of fabric in the back of your stash. This is a good place to hide it. Be sure that the "odd piece of fabric" won't show through your top fabrics.

Cut the vest or jacket bodice patterns out of foundation fabric. Pin together at shoulder and side seams, then fit. When you have a good fit, mark the front and back side seams, with magic marker. If the garment design needs to match at the side seams, you must fit with the foundation fabric, as an exact match cannot be made if you try to take it in later. The side seam design areas will be distorted. See "Out of Africa" on pages 39-40 for excellent illustration of this point.

For perfect sizing, use the foundation fabric as the pattern for your wearable. You know it's going to fit!

Skirt Borders

When creating your own special wearables, **don't forget the border of your skirt**. To create the following skirt designs, you need to be working with a straight skirt pattern with no curved seams. You can utilize any traditional quilt block on the border of your skirt. First decide how many blocks you want around the bottom including the design you want to use. Ten to twelve inch blocks are good sizes for skirt borders. The finished width of your skirt should be at least 60", although 72" is ideal.

The next step involves your dress or jumper pattern. Hold the pattern up to your body, and pin it at the shoulder and secure in front. Next, with someone's help, measure from the seam allowance at the bottom of the bodice to desired the skirt length (see #1). Next, assemble the number of blocks desired and join them together. (see second illustration)

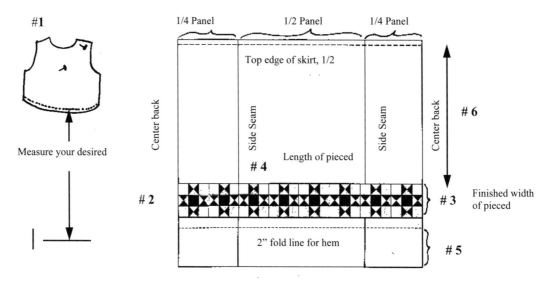

Measure the finished <u>width</u> of the pieced block section: **# 2 =** _____. Measure the <u>length</u> of the pieced block section: **#4 =** _____. The lower border on the bottom of your skirt is 6" wide and is cut the same length as your pieced block section. Sew the lower border to the bottom edge of the pieced block section, using a 1/4" a seam allowance. Measure down 2" from top of lower border. This will be your hem line (see #5).

<u>Length to cut Skirt Panels:</u> Take finished skirt length and subtract 2" from it and the width of your pieced strip. Add 3/4" for seam allowances and you will have the length you need to cut the upper portion of your skirt (see #6). For example:

Finished length of skirt	36 " (example)
<u>Subtract</u> 2" Bottom Border	- 2 "
<u>Subtract</u> finished Width of Pieced Strip	<u>-12 "</u> (example)
	= 22"
* Add 3/4 " for seam allowance	<u>+ 3/4"</u>
Length to cut skirt panels	22 3/4"

* This 3/4" allows for 1/4" to stitch to pieced block section and 1/2" for top seam allowance.

Divide the finished width *(#4)* of your skirt into fourths. Don't forget to add seam allowances. Your skirt back section will each be 1/4 of the skirt width and the front panel will be 1/2 of the width of skirt measurement. On the back panels add a seam allowance to the center back and sides. To the front section add only seam allowance to sides seams. Sew these sections together.

I recommend that you **line your skirt** so all raw edges are enclosed. It is worth the extra effort. The <u>width</u> of the fabric is figured as above. When the skirt is assembled turn it up at the 2" marking line. The <u>length</u> at which you will need to cut your lining is the distance from the raw hem edge to the top of the skirt, plus 1". Cut the lining and sew the side seams together. With the right sides together and the side and back seams matching, sew the lining to the raw hem edge of the skirt. Turn the lining so that the underside of the lining and skirt are together. Baste the top edges together. A 1/2" Seam Allowance is allowed on this edge.

Fabric Selection.....................Let the fun begin!

After your equipment is in order, your pattern is selected, and traced and perhaps modified, the next step is in the Process is to select just the perfect fabrics for your project. Never cut the fabrics until they have been prepared for the job for which they are intended.

Fabric Type, Don't Limit Yourself.

When selecting types of fabrics to use for your wearables, do not limit yourself to using only cottons. Try satins, silks, lames, decorator fabrics, leather, or whatever catches your eye.Try different color schemes or designs and look at everything as a possibility in your wearables.

Since 1995 when I first published "Creative Techniques for Wearables" fabric choices have grown tremendously. The older companies that were fashion fabric companies when I owned my fabric store are now in the premium cotton business. It was either change or die. Fortunately, new companies have emerged on the scene, including Free Spirit, founded by Donna Wilder, the originator of the Fairfield Fashion Show. Donna has found wonderful designers and they offer truly unique fabrics. To my eye, they are wonderful.

Fabric Selection

For Pieced Projects: When I use pieced blocks in my projects, I enjoy watching the detailed blocks come to life with the care of deciding exactly where to place a particular motif in a wonderful piece of fabric. In other words , "fussy cutting". For a simple illustration see page 63. Most often the fabrics I select for a project are jewel tones.

To create dynamic pieced blocks, it is important to use a dramatic background fabric. For years, quilters used white or muslin as the background fabric for their work. It was readily available and worked with all color schemes. I would never criticize the great Baltimore quilts or the fabulous antique quilts made many years ago, but I feel the quilts being made today; using bold and dynamic background fabric, are more visually appealing and stimulating.

Always choose your background fabric with a critical eye. A light motif on a dark background tends to draw too much attention to the lighter color; it distracts from the other colors in the project. Further, I never choose background fabric with more than two colors, and the dark one must dominate.

Since 1994, I have used six bolts of a black-with-gold-stars fabric from Speigel. Unfortunately it is no longer available. I never imagined that I would use this fabric so frequently, but it simply kept calling me back again and again. Vivid colors bounced off the black and gave life and vitality to my creations.

Long ago, I made an important discovery about fabric color design: tone-on-tone fabrics. They give more visual texture and interest to the finished project than do solids, yet they speak in the piece as a solid.

Further, you might consider using various patterns of similar-color tone-on-tones in your project. For example, on my "Christmas Dress" pattern, red tone-on-tone fabric was used as the background fabric for the tree blocks. Instead of using the same fabric for all blocks, each is a different red tone-on-tone and the look is much more interesting. Try this and you'll see what I mean. See page 45.

Types of Fabrics to use for Wearables: As I mentioned in the first paragraph of this page, I enjoy using all types of fabrics. At this time; silk Dupioni is at the top. Other ideas are:

- Ethnic fabrics, panels and trims, molas, hamong handwork, and batik panels
- Decorator fabrics, animal prints and coordinates
- A collection of neutral tones
- Bali cotton prints coordinated with batik panels
- Silks that have a lot of body. I love working with Dupioni, as it handles so well.
- A collection of lightweight suitings coordinated with tapestry that have ethnic or animal designs.
- A collection of fabrics for a holiday jacket, here again tapestries with velveteens, satins, silks, and wools.
- Hand-dyed cottons such as suede cottons from Cherrywood
- A country look using Debbie Mumm-type fabrics for a holiday jacket. I made a Christmas jacket using her Santa Sampler Wallhanging pattern just for the Santa's. I had to modify them a little to fit on the jacket. See page 45.
- Patterns with angels, snowmen, a gardening theme, or whatever is your favorite.

Fabric Preparation
Pre-wash to Set Colors
It is a good idea to set dark colors when mixing lights and darks. To do this, mix 1 cup vinegar and 1/4 cup dissolved salt. Add this mixture to your clothes washer, using warm water.

To test whether you should set color, stitch together small strips of dark and light fabrics. Soak in warm water to see if the colors run; if they do, you can be assured they will do the same in your finished project. Soak and rinse, rinse, rinse the dark fabric until no more dye is in the rinse water. If the color will not set, consider changing to a different fabric. (The recipe above also works to set the color of new jeans or other clothing

Pre-wash to Prevent Shrinkage
Always prewash and dry fabrics to take out any shrinkage. Even with the best fabrics, shrinkage can be a real problem; and can shrink 2-3 inches in width and an inch or more in length. Always buy extra fabric. Remember, the shrinkage problem is not the fault of your fabric store; it's the nature of the beast!

Drying your Fabrics
First, machine dry your fabric to achieve maximum shrinkage but select a heat setting that will not damage your fabrics. Once the garment is complete, I suggest you line dry. This ensures that your fabric colors remain bright and beautiful.

It is amazing what a nice breeze will do for fabrics or clothing hung on a clothes line. Heat from a dryer has a way of dulling colors, I hang dry whenever I can. When it's too cold to hang outside, clothes are hung in my utility room. This happens, even with quality home dryers.

To reduce wrinkling, use a good, quality fabric softener when washing the garment.

Stain Removal:
One option is to use a product called UN-DO. It is a clear liquid in a clear spray bottle with red printing. I usually spray it on a white cotton ball and rub the cotton on the stain. If the fabric is washable or if there is a lot of blood, I spray directly on the stain and rub. Sometimes it takes several times if the stain is either really bad or old. Also, I have used my fingernail to get into ridges, if the fabric has that kind of weave. I have even gotten out red lipstick out of the front of a formal. What a panic!!!! Also, if the fabric is silk or satin that might ring with water, I stipple the moisture to the outer edge of the ring until it disappears. This avoids a ring. Even if I am not that careful, I haven't had a problem with this product making a ring. I have even used the iron to dry the outer portion of the wet area. Do not put the iron on the stain itself or it will set the stain. I have also heard that hydrogen peroxide, with a little soap or detergent, will do the same thing. As with all things, try a sample first.

Courtesy of Ilaine Hartman of New Orleans, LA
Couturier, Costumer,
Fairfield Fashion Show designer/participant,
President Elect of Gulf States Quilting Association
Charter member of Contemporary Fiber Artists of LA.

Burn test for fiber content
Being the "Fabriholics" that we are, do you ever pull a piece of fabric from your stash and have no any idea about the correct fiber content? This happens especially with fashion fabrics.

- Cut a small piece of your fabric and place in an ash tray. Light it on fire with a match. Be careful as your fabric may flare up. Different fabrics react differently to fire; the list below will help you define the fiber content of your fabric.
- **SILK** burns to a fine ash and smells like burnt chicken feathers.
- **WOOL** burns to a fine ash and smells like burnt hair.
- **SYNTHETICS** leave a hard residue, they resemble shriveled plastic.
- **ACETATE RAYONS** will dissolve when soaked in nail polish remover.
- **BLENDS** are too difficult to identify accurately.

(Courtesy of Diane Womack of Arkansas)

Home Decorator Department
An Uncommon Source
Don't overlook the Home Decorator Department of your favorite fabric store when looking for wearable trims and fabrics. Always check the laundering procedure for your purchase and pre shrink fabric and trims.

Friendly Reminder: Never wear make-up when working on white or light color fabrics.

Even though this information is written with Wearables in mind, it can be applied to all sewing and quilting projects!

Notes........ Your ideas.............from the Internet..........

Ladies..."start your rotary cutters".....

The next step in the process is cutting our fabric selections. What design are you going to use for this step? Following are simple piecing ideas that make for interesting Wearables or Quilts. They serve as the base design foundation for your project, upon which you can apply pieced blocks, appliqué or other embellishments or simply leave as they are.

Planned Scrap Backgrounds.........................

I am intrigued when I hear Quilter's discuss making scrap quilts; where hundreds of fabrics are used in a project. In workshop situations, scraps squares are often traded for a larger selection, this is good idea, because you end up with more fabrics in your design.

One suggestion is to place all your scrap fabrics in a large paper bag and draw out the fabrics that will be used, not giving any thought to the color or pattern. I could never do that. Even when I use several hundred fabrics in one project, each print is selected with care and auditioned for the project. There are fabrics I don't like because of color or design. To be true to myself, I can not place these fabrics in my project. I must "love them" or they will never be used. All fabrics, whatever the shape are placed on my design wall; then I step back and view the overall appearance of the collection. I ask myself, "is one fabric sticking out from the others," the pink elephant fabric is cute but...better take it out or I may not be happy with the end results.

My goal in this type of project is to create a gorgeous collage` of fabrics. It will be a planned scrap background for my wearable or quilt.

How big a section do I piece?

First decide on the size shape or block you need in your project. An 3 1/2" square is a good cutting size, the same would be true for strips of fabric. This size will allow for the use of many different fabrics, but not so many as to be over whelming.

To determine how large your pieced sections need to be, you need to make a muslin so that you have the correct fit for your garment. See page 18.

Measure your muslin sections to see how big a piece needs to be made to cover each section.

For the example to the left, the width of the pattern section is 54". The length is 36"

If you plan to use a **finished** 3" square,

divide 3 into the width and length of the area to be pieced.

54" ÷ 3 = 18 squares across
36" ÷ 3 = 12 squares down

Next multiply
18 squares x 12 squares = 216 squares
The same idea applies to the number of finished blocks needed for a project.

Remember: this will only cover either the front or back or your garment. If it's a jacket there will be sleeves.

It's play time- - - take the 216 squares and arrange them on your design wall. Step back..........move several around......... look good?.........next take to your machine and stitch.

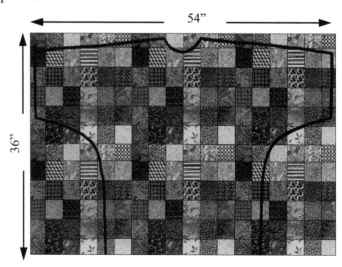

Scrap Squares

Construction of this back-ground is very simple. The fantastic appearance comes in the selection of as many fabrics as possible. Remember to pick each one carefully. I suggest you cut 3 1/2" squares. that will be set square.

Along with my large selection of fabrics, I choose prints that can be fussy cut. Fussy cutting is selecting a certain motif within a print, then cutting the fabric so that the motif is in the center of the square or whatever shape you're using. See illustrations to the right, below and "Tis the Season" on page 45.

Other Uses for Scrap Squares

Off Set Scrap Squares

On Point Scrap Squares

See "Patchwork Splendeur Jacket and "Sunrise, Sunset" on page 46

Scrap Strips

For this Background, cut 3" x 6"- 8" strips of fabric. Area to be covered will determine the number to be cut. See "Eye of the Tiger" page 54.

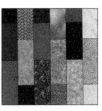

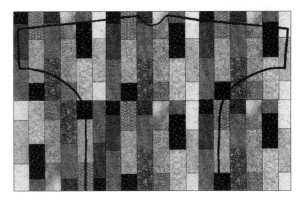

Scrap Triangles

The background of my 20th Anniversary Fairfield ensemble "Arabesque"(page 76) is fabric triangles. Because of the large area to be covered, 6" triangles were cut. The same size was cut for the sleeveless coat, "Bali Maiden" (page 46). Both garments are an amazing collection of fabrics; but the scrap background was only as dynamic as the two to three hundred fabrics I selected. Most of the fabrics were from fabric club samples, which helped to keep my cost down. See more information on next page about fabric club samples.

Fussy Cut Triangles

Triangles are fun to "Fussy Cut. I buy fabric with fish motifs so they can swim through my designs. Remember the triangles will fit together as illustrated; keep this in mind when placing a bird, fish, or other character in your piece, you don't have the fish swimming upside down.

Notice the difference it makes if you turn the stripe in a different direction. Template for the triangle is on page 69.

Fabric Club Samples

If you belong to a Fabric Club, save all of your samples. To work for the following, they should be at least 4" square. Sort them into color families. At least half of the triangles in Arabesque were cut from these samples,  thus giving me so many more fabrics without having to purchase more fabric.

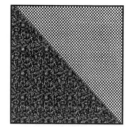
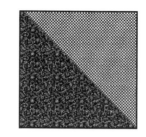

What to do with all those fabric samples?

Making Right Triangles with Fabric Samples 4" Square or larger

This method works best with large fabric samples, at least 4" square. Be sure and check for accuracy.

A simple formula to determine how large to cut squares for this quick piece method is to add 7/8" to the finished size of the square.

Place light sample on top of dark sample, right sides together.

A. Draw a visible line from corner to corner.

Right Triangle squares using strong background fabric

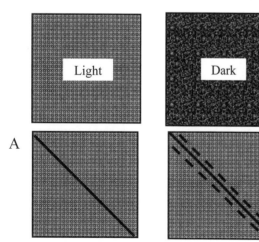

B. Stitch on both sides of this line 1/4 " seam allowance. Cut on marked line, open and you have two right triangle squares. Press seam allowance to one side.

Right Triangle squares with light background fabric

Putting it All Together.............

Sweatshirt Foundation

A sweatshirt is a great foundation for a quilted jacket. It serves as both pattern and batting. My jacket patterns are made on a sweatshirt foundation. I wear a size 12, but, I purchase a man's 2X sweatshirt for my jackets. This is so I have longer length in the body and sleeves, because all ribbing is cut off except at the neck.

My technique for making a jacket includes cutting apart the sweatshirt. I do this for several reasons:
1. To have a flat working surface,
2. So that the sweatshirt can be fit
3. So pockets can be included in the size seams.

Following are the basic instructions for making a quilted sweatshirt foundation jacket. You can apply any of the planned scrap quilt ideas, your favorite blocks or appliqué to a sweatshirt jacket. Put on your "thinking caps", I bet you come up with several good ideas for a new project.

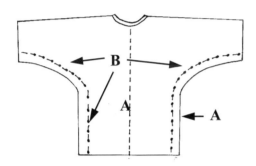

Wash and dry sweatshirt. Cut off bottom and cuff ribbing. **Do not** cut off Neck Ribbing.

A. Center Front and Side Seams

As illustrated find center front and side seam areas on sweatshirt. Do this on a flat surface; lay your sweatshirt flat, allowing side seam fold to form. Most sweatshirt are made in a tube with no side seams. Be sure your sweatshirt is laying straight and even, measure from side seam area to side seam area. Divide amount in half and this should be center front. Double Check...when you're sure it's correct, mark along center front and side seam folds. Carefully cut open center front; then up side seam folds, continuing on up under sleeve seam until sweatshirt side and sleeve seams are cut open.

B. Fit the Sweatshirt

The following is for those who purchase a larger size sweatshirt than usual. Pin up side seams and sleeves. You may want to taper the sleeve toward the cuff edge.

(approximately 10-12" across as it will most likely be wider. Pin the jacket to a loose but not baggy fit, as you would a straight cut jacket. Cut off extra sweatshirt fabric along side and sleeve seams, leaving 5/8" seam allowance.

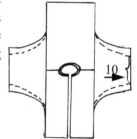

Sleeve

For approximate sleeve length, pin in shoulder pads if you are using them as the pads will make a difference in length. Try on the jacket, measure for sleeve length, then add two inches for good measure. Cut off extra sweatshirt sleeve fabric.

C. Cut Open Sweatshirt

Place your cut open sweatshirt on a large working area, spreading it out until it is flat. Work at arranging your pieced sections on the sweatshirt. This illustration will give you an idea of how big a section to piece each jacket section: fronts, sleeves and back.

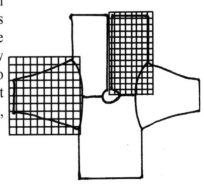

Pieced Sections

Lay the finished pieced sections on top of your sweatshirt to see if it covers completely. There will be two front sections, one back section and two sleeve sections.

D. When you place your pieced sections over your sweatshirt, line up the bottom of your pieced sections with the bottom of the front and back sweatshirt, remembering the pieced sections need to cover the shoulder seam at the top of the pieced section. Make sure center fronts are the same length.

And what do we spy on Jenny's 40"x72" cutting mat, her Grabbit.

Shoulder seam

Fold front and back pieced sections along shoulder seam or seam area of sweatshirt. Press along this line. Be very accurate. Leave about 1" folded under and trim away excess fabric. Lap the front section over the back, slipping unfolded back section under front, then pin in place.

Sleeve Sections

While flat, fit pieced sections on each sleeve, leaving sweatshirt flat as before. Line up on sweatshirt sleeve cuff edge. Fold under 1/4" along both bodice sections next to sleeve sections. Pin this fold line. Slide top of sleeve section under edge of front and back sections. Trim excess from sleeve section under front and back. Trim sleeve sections to fit sweatshirt when you are sure all is correct. Pin or baste the outside edge.

Front section

Sleeve section

Back section

F. Neck edge

Find the groove between the jacket and neck ribbing. I feel for this grove with my fingers. Mark this line on front and back top patch sections with pins. Be very accurate. Mark away from pin line 1/4". Cut along this line.

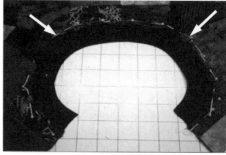

Fold under 1/4 inch and pin in place around neck. Pin right in the groove. Stitch shoulder seam, back, fronts and sleeves with .004 nylon thread, so that the stitching lines will not show.

Basting

Use .004 nylon thread machine to baste sections to sweatshirt. Stitch in the ditch about every two rows. This is important so that your fabrics don't slip around on top of the stretchy sweatshirt fabric.

Embellishing

Embellish your jacket with machine quilting, designer threads and yarns, whatever your heart desires. For many ideas see pages 82-104.

G. Pocket

Cut 4 - 7" X 9" medium weight fabric section that matches the color of sweatshirt. Finish edges of sections and apply to sweatshirt as illustrated using a 1/4" seam allowance.

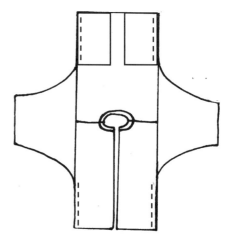

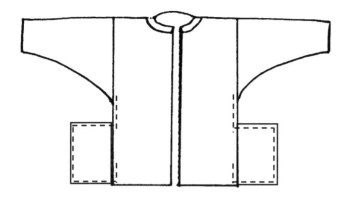

(H) - Sew side, sleeve and pocket seams using 5/8" seam allowance.

(I) Turn pocket so that it lays on the inside of the front section. Pin in place along seam allowance. Turn over to the front, where pins show through from the underside, mark this

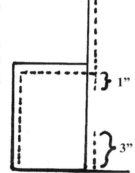

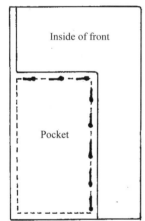

with a pen that disappears or a chalk one that can be brushed away. Take pins out from below and stabilize the pocket with pins on top.

Thread your sewing machine with .004 nylon thread. In the bobbin, thread to match your sweatshirt. Stitch on marked lines. By using the nylon thread, the stitching line will disappear. Use smoke nylon on dark fabrics and the clear on light.

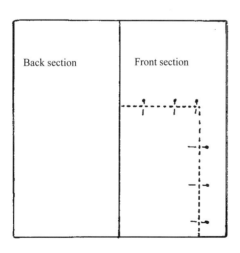

Center Front Finishes

1. Bias binding for center front, lower and sleeve edge. Measure these areas, then add a little. There are two options for the bias binding.

   A. Bias strips out of main fabric 2 1/4" wide. Fold and press.

   B. Multi-colored bias binding, see page 115.

   Apply bias to center front, lower and sleeve edge, the same as you would bind a quilt. I apply the bias to under side first and lap to machine stitch down on top. Miter Corners and finish off the top ends by tucking in a small amount of bias. Often when I stitch down the bias, I couch designer thread along this sewing line. Close with Custom Frogs see page 116.

2. Cut two strips of fabric 2" wide and interface. Stitch along center front opening. Fold back and press, finished off the ends. You can now apply separating Zipper, following package directions. Remember to finish the bottom edge of your jacket either with bias binding or a small turned up hem.

Shoulder Pads

My shoulders are wimpy and with a jacket this bulky I need a good lift or I look sad. I suggest at least a 1/2" finished raglan shoulder pad. Stitch in place with hand quilting thread.

Knit Collar (Optional)

Use a purchased knit collar, embellished with couched designer thread in a swirl design and it looks wonderful. Try stitching along the edge of the collar with a decorative stitch on your machine for additional interest. See page 102 for more information on collars.

Stitch collar to the very top edge of jacket neck ribbing, about 1/4" down. Center about 1" from center front on each side. Pin baste in place.

Use a zigzag stitch with the collar on top. Use thread the color of the collar in the top thread, thread the color of the neck ribbing in the bobbin.

Using Traditional Quilt Blocks To Create Wearables

Make two blocks of the same pattern. For examples, two-12 1/2" blocks will be illustrated. One set square, the other on point to be the front and back focal points. See Denim Star on page 45.

Front Block

The front block needs to be cut in half as illustrated.When choosing a commercial pattern, select one with straight lines, no darts. If there is a back seam, eliminate by placing back seam line on fold of fabric.

Be sure of correct sizing before proceeding.

Fabric - I suggest using the same fabric for the vest, as the background sections of your block. This will make your block design float.

A. Take a 12 x 12 piece of paper and pretend it is your block for drafting purposes. Your actual fabric block will be 12 1/2 " Square.Lay the piece of paper square or on point on front and back pattern pieces as shown. Secure with scotch tape.

B. As shown on the drawing, create new pattern sections front and back as the broken lines illustrate. Cut these sections apart and trace pattern pieces adding 1/4" seam allowance to sides that are marked with an X

Mark grainline on your new pattern piece.

Cut main sections of vest with new pattern pieces

Sew front and back sections together.

Add batting to vest sections if you desire..

Hand or machine quilt

Let your quilted fronts and back be your pattern for cutting out the lining.

Sew together the shoulder seams and side seams of both quilted sections and lining. Baste raw edges together: armholes, neck, front and hem.

- Use a bias binding to finish as you would your favorite quilt. See page 115.

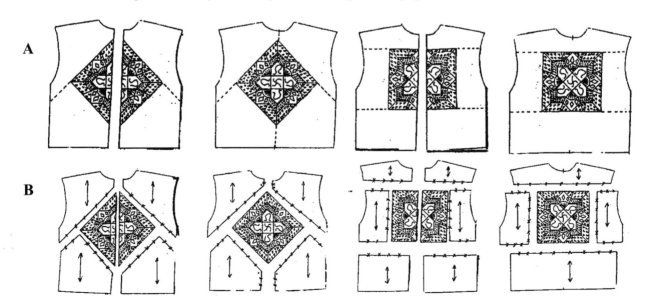

Overall Quilt Designs for Wearables...................

Another technique to use in making wearables is to piece an overall quilt design for the front and back, such as Trip Around The World, Log Cabin Blocks, Lover's Knot, or Hidden Wells. Measure the area it will take to complete cover your pattern sections. It's the same idea as making a wall hanging size quilt, except that you turn it into a vest or jacket. For a sleeve you would do the same thing. See page 45 for garment examples.

 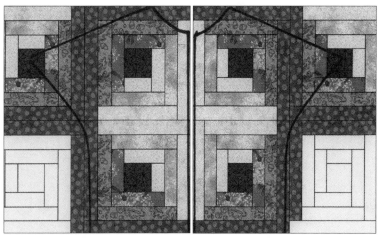

Set Ideas for One Piece Jackets......................

See "Hidden Wells" Jacket on page 45.

There are many good jacket patterns on the market. They all consist of fronts, back, sleeves and often a sleeve gusset. This can be changed, so you can use this idea for making a one-piece jacket. The sleeve and arm hole of the bodice sections must be straight set as illustrated. On a flat surface, lay the pattern pieces so that seam lines overlap. Tape the paper pieces together to create one large pattern piece. Make a muslin to check for correct sizing.

After you know you have a correct fit, gauge the number of blocks necessary to make your jacket.

See page 28 for information on how to figure the number of blocks needed for a project.

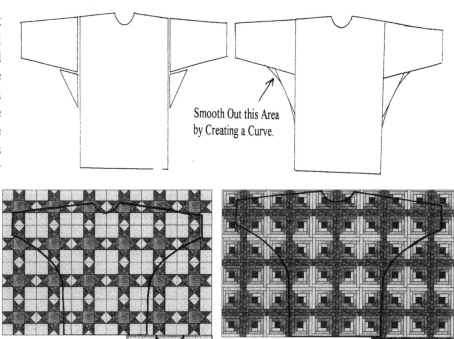

Smooth Out this Area by Creating a Curve.

Design Concepts for Wearables.......................

On the following pages are design ideas for many of the garments I've created over the years. I'm sorry there are no patterns, but it's not possible with a book such as this. Select a commercial pattern close to what I used, modify the pattern with the sketches and design to your hearts content.

Silks and Satins Log Cabin Vest

Color Picture Page 45.

This vest was made from Log Cabin Blocks. For this short version I used four blocks for the front and four for the back. Remember when designing with Log Cabin you must work in 4s to get a complete design. This vest has an off the shoulder design, so another block may be needed on the outside of the top blocks as illustrated. If a longer version is needed, you need sixteen blocks for the length. This design definitely has a center and you will need to keep that in mind.

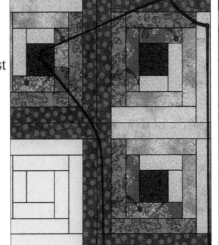

This vest was made from assorted silks, tapestry and velveteen.

To calculate how large each block must be, mark block on pattern as illustrated below.

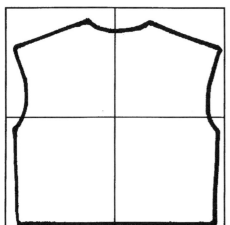

Always let the design of the blocks be your lead. Lay the bottom edge of your vest pattern, along the bottom edge of the pieced section as illustrated. If you use 1/4" seam allowances on center front you will loose very little of your block design.

After you cut out the vest front section, mark 5/8" seam allowance at shoulder and side seams. Next mark the design intersection for shoulder and side seams on front and back. This is where my extra long, sewing pins come in handy. These reference marks are made at seam allowance because this is where the match will take place. With effort a near perfect match can be achieved, you may need to "unch" just a little.

Trip Around the World Vest

Color Picture Page 45

This short vest was made from assorted wool fabrics in shade of red, black and dark gray. I varied from the usual Trip Around the World quilt design in that I cut rectangles instead of squares.

Trace your pattern onto paper and draw the squares or rectangles. This will give you the number of squares or rectangles to cut or follow the formula on page 28. Remember to center this design on vest fronts and back.

On the front you will cut the pieced section in half down the center. Use

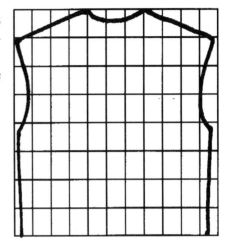

If you like the shape of these two vests - they are the same as my pattern, "Jenny's Vest", which can be ordered from me. See www.jennyraymond.com - Catalog page.

1/4" seam allowance, so as little of the design is lost as possible.

Always let the design of the blocks be your lead. Lay pieced section along the bottom edge of your vest pattern.

After you cut out the vest front section, mark 5/8" seam allowance at shoulder and side seams. Next mark the design intersection for shoulder and side seams on front and back. This is where my extra long, sewing pins come in handy. These reference marks are made at seam allowance because this is where the match will take place. With effort a near perfect match can be achieved, you may need to "unch" just a little.

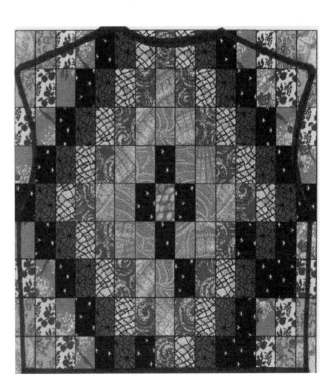

Leather & Lace

Color picture on page 54.

These ensemble was designed for the 1995 Nebraska Cattlebaron's Ball Fashion Show. The ensemble features mocha colored lace in a blouse and three tiered skirt, along with a vest made from several shades of brown leather, chocolate moiré, ecru lace and lace appliqués, ecru rayon fringe and white pearls.

Leather

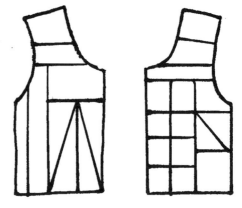

For years there was a box of leather scraps in my basement, waiting for a design to come to mind. I finally pulled it out and "Leather and Lace" is the result. To create a vest similar to this one follow these steps:

- Cut a foundation fabric of your vest pattern. Mark on the front foundation with permanent magic marker the illustrated patch design.
- Use a sharp rotary cutter and cut the patch sections. 4-5 different shades of brown leather were used. For a different look, use the wrong side of the leather. Cutting leather will "feel" different. Practice on a scrap or two.
- Place the patch section on the foundation, butting all edges. Use a glue stick to hold the patches in place. Stitch in place with a leather machine needle, nylon thread and a zigzag stitch. (Try a sample first.) Much to my amazement, I didn't have any problems butting and stitching the leather patch's.

Lace

When I had the Sewing Basket, it had a large bridal department and we stocked many special order books. One had lace motifs, trims and yard goods. Samples from one of these books were used for this vest. I machine stitched the lace motifs and trim in place on the vest form.

Vest Back

The vest back was cut in four layers.
1. The back vest section was cut from chocolate moiré satin.
2. Scalloped mocha lace was cut to fall 3/4 length of the back.
3. At center top back a large lace piece was used, one that might be used for the neck of a bridal gown.
4. Another section of lace is the final layer.

If you study the picture of the back, you'll see what types of lace were used. It was stabilized at all edges except for the second scalloped edge, this I left loose.

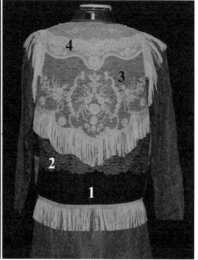

I sewed all the pearls on by hand with hand quilting thread. This was hard to do as the leather was not easy to penetrate with my sewing needle. Sewer's Aid might help with this problem. The vest was lined and bias bound in the mocha lace. The silky rayon fringe was sewn on by machine.

Out of Africa Vest

Color Picture page 46

Fabrics

wool/blends (light weight suitings),
corduroy, suede cloth, velveteen
and a decorator tapestry.

Fabric Requirements

- 1 yd. Tapestry
- 1/4 yd. each of several different suiting blends, suede cloth, corduroy, velveteen
- 2 -3 yd. each of five or six different woven trims, braids, ribbons. These need to be at least 1/2" wide.
- 1 great button for front closure
- Assorted buttons to embellish vest.
- Large snaps
- Fusible interfacing
- Lining, amt. pattern calls for
- Foundation Fabric - Amount pattern calls for.
- Black Sharpie Felt Pen, 24" Quilt Ruler, Rotary Cutter with Sharp Blade, Mat

KWIK SEW 2731 was used for this vest. I selected this pattern because of it's shape.

A front lap closure was designed for this vest resembling a rhino horn. This extension is added to the right front and should be right at, or a little below, you waistline. See page 116.

Cut the vest out of foundation fabric, then check for fit. It is important that you have a good fit now. After pinning and fitting, mark side seams on both fronts and back with magic marker. Don't skip this step. I marked the exact side seams on the foundation so that I could correctly match the strips of fabric as illustrated below.

The areas where I placed the tapestry are large in size and shape and were determined by the design I wanted to emphasis in tapestry.

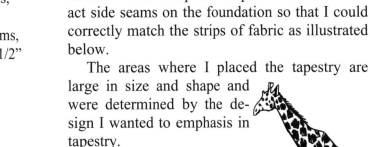

The areas that were strip pieced can vary as well. The finished widths of these strips varied from 2"-3 1/2".

(Continued on the next page)

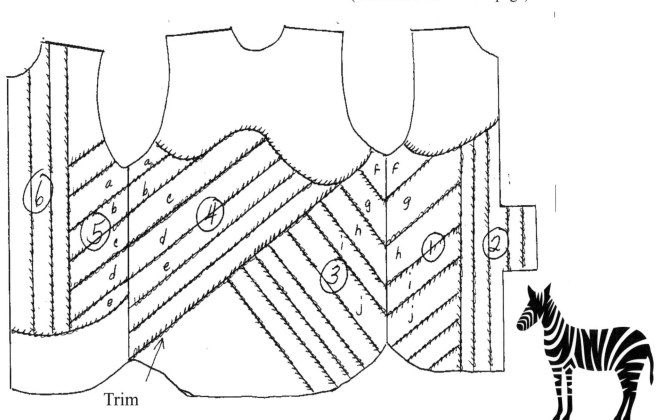

Trim

1. Machine baste the foundation vest fronts and back together at marked side seams. Accurately draw all lines on foundation as illustrated in drawing. Be sure to draw matching sections the same width. Ex. (a & a) (b & b). Take out machine basting. This step is done because when matching at seams, the match is at the stitching line, not the outside edge. Lay the vest sections side by side after you take out the basting, now you can see the importance of correct fit at this point, the lines don't match up.

2. Decide the order of your fabrics and then cut according to width of the   section it will occupy. Add 5/8" to each section for seam allowance. This   allows   a little for "turn" of the heavier fabrics.

3. Allow 1/4" seam allowance and strip piece; stitch the sections (1-6) in the order suggested on page   If you stitch in order you will be able to enclose all raw edges. These are numbered 1-6.

4. Machine quilt over the pieced sections (1-6) of this vest. I used a 4.0 Double Needle and solid rayon thread.   In the same sections, couch designer threads.

5. Next stitch down the trims and braids over the stitching lines. The braid will go over the top of the designer threads.

6. Position the tapestry and pin baste in place. Do not machine quilt on tapestry as it will detract from the scene.

7. Cover the raw edges of the tapestry with the braids used as embellishment.

8. Press well.

9. Pockets - if you want to add pockets see page 32.

10. Stitch together side seams, being exact with matching strips.

11. Lining the vest: cut lining from finished back and front sections. Place right sides of vest sections on right side of lining. Cut with right sides together. I used the envelope method. (page 119)

12. If desired, embellish with additional buttons, charms etc. I made a gorgeous button and bead bouquet on the left shoulder. See pages 95.

Front closure to vest with wooden elephant button. Closure is in the shape of a Rhino horn.

The Glitzy Chicken

Color Picture Page 54

This vest was made for the "Fowl Frolic" challenge during one of eleanor peace bailey's visits to Nebraska. The challenge was to make anything we wanted as long as it had a chicken theme. The "Fowl Frolic" was a money-raising event for the Quilt Preservation Committee of the Nebraska State Quilt Guild. The evening was a "hoot", rather a "cluck". A friend went with me and we had a great time. We rented a chicken costume that she wore. My "pet" chicken was on a leash and we went around the hall with a bucket of candy corn to feed the participants. It was great because no one could figure out who the chicken was. Anyway back to the vest.

Below is the basic design for the front and back. Simple design idea, mostly strip piecing, that could be implemented with any fabric design theme. It was embellished with sequin trim, jewels applied with Aileene's Jewel It and miscellaneous buttons.

Bali Maiden Sleeveless Coat

Color Picture on page 46.

This calf length sleeveless coat is a great example of a modified pattern. There was not a collar on this pattern so I drew and created what I wanted. To do this kind of modifying you need pattern drawing paper or fabric on which to draw the new collar and front collar panel.

The coat was made using triangles as the background design. The focus of the coat is a great Bali Batik Panel down the back. I used part of the panel for the collar and the rest down the back. It was, of course, a long straight piece of fabric but I decided that it was boring to just use the straight line of the panel. I followed the design in the panel and cut a jagged edge along the design. I like what happened. The panel was stitched on top of the triangle background using a wide satin stitch and Sulky Metallic thread. It was embellished with double needle machine quilting—designer threads and continuous prairie points were used as a trim around the collar and front lapel. See page 104 on continuous prairie points. The edges are finished with bias binding.

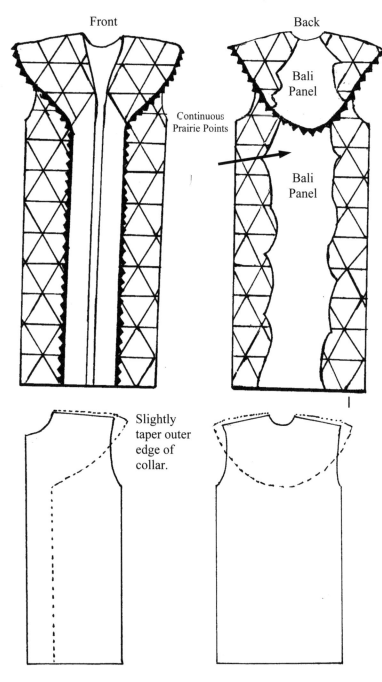

Front

Back

Bali Panel

Continuous Prairie Points

Bali Panel

Slightly taper outer edge of collar.

Pattern Modification for Collar

Below is an illustration of how to include a collar on a pattern that does not have one. The shoulder edge of the collar must be slopped at a different degree than the shoulder seam of the vest, as illustrated. The outside edge of the collar shoulder seam should turn down ever so slightly, so that the collar doesn't stick out straight. You will need to cut a muslin of your design and see how it lays on the vest pattern and off the edge of your shoulder. Be sure to allow ease on the neck edge.

This collar includes a lapel that goes the full length of the coat.

I laid pattern tracing fabric or paper on top of my vest pattern and drew the collar as illustrated by the dotted lines. This may take some practice and work, but after a while, it will feel natural. Once again I suggest you make a muslin of your collar design, then pin baste to your main garment, this way if it doesn't fit correctly, you can make adjustments before you cut your fabric.

Eye of the Tiger............*here kitty, kitty.*
Color Picture on page 54

Eye of the Tiger is a design that can be made using many different types of fabrics. The starting point for this jacket was the great tiger print used for the yokes and sleeves.

Select a pattern similar to the one in the drawing.

Fabrics:
Main Fabric 1 3/4 yd. This is an average and could vary according to the pattern you select.
10-15 coordinating fabrics. Fat quarters work great. The lower section is a "Planned Scrap" project. You will cut the fabric as on page 29.
Lining and Foundation Fabric: amount pattern calls for.

Your pattern will need to be modified to include a large yoke. This is where you will showcase your "one great print". Leave a good size area for the planned scrap part of the jacket. See page 20 information on pattern modification.

Embellishments: After the fronts, back and sleeves are assembled, machine quilt in your favorite style, then embellish with designer threads. A woven braid was sewn along the lower edge of the yoke and around the neck
and down the front. Black tear drop beads were sewn to the braid along the yoke, giving the idea of fringe. Hand sewing these beads in place was a timely project, but well worth it because of the results. Below is an illustration of how the beads appear.

Finishing: Cut and sew lining using the original patterns sections. You can finish with an envelope lining or plain bias binding or multi-colored bias as illustrated on page 115.. If you finish with the bias binding, remember to place wrong sides of garments and lining together. Baste these edges, then apply the bias. For closures select either a separating zipper or frog closures as illustrated on page 116.

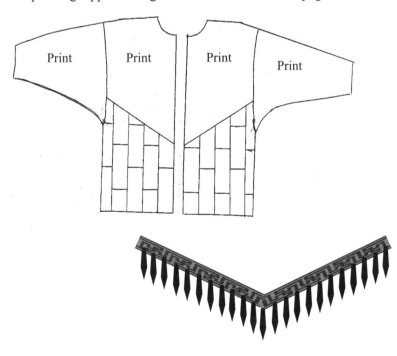

Notes.........Your ideas.............from the Internet...........

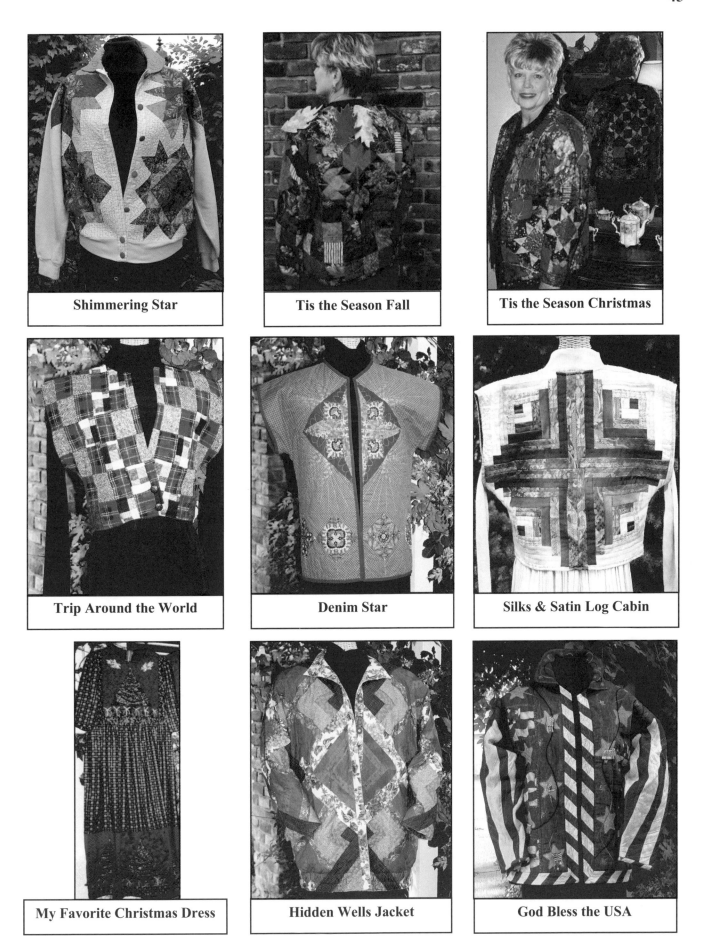

Shimmering Star

Tis the Season Fall

Tis the Season Christmas

Trip Around the World

Denim Star

Silks & Satin Log Cabin

My Favorite Christmas Dress

Hidden Wells Jacket

God Bless the USA

Sand Hills Melody

Garden of Eden

Silk Flower Shadow Applique

I Love Santa

Out of Africa

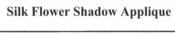

Patchwork Splendeur

Sunrise Sunset

Bali Maiden

Fabriqué Furr

This technique of layering, stitching and slashing fabrics has been around for a long time. My name for this technique is "Fabrique Fur" but the more common name is chenille. It is a sandwich of fabrics. The bottom fabric serves as the foundation for the project, the in between fabrics (from 3-5 layers) are the filling, and next is the top layer. This technique can be used on wearables and quilts alike. This is an easy technique, but one that takes time.

The steps to create a "Fabrique Fur" project are:

*   Decide on the number of layers you want in your project. I suggest at least 5 for the whole sandwich.
*   Purchase 5 times the amount of fabric called for in your pattern. ****Read about my good buy on 60" cotton on the next page. This would be a good place to bury "ugly fabrics" in your stash if the colors are right.
*   Preshrink and press all fabrics (see page 26 on preshrinking)
*   Layer your fabric selections.
*   Mark stitching lines as illustrated using a 24" quilt ruler. I mark the stitching lines 1" apart, when I use cotton fabrics. Stitch through all 5+ layers using at least a size 14 needle. For the fabric to fur when slashed, the stitching lines must be on some what of a bias marking line.
*   The stitching can be done two ways: normal machine stitching or a decorator thread couched in a narrow zigzag stitch. The decorator threads add color and sparkle to the project.

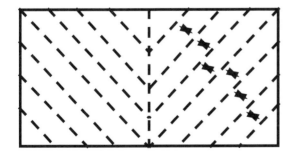

*   Slashing between the stitching lines is next. Very important fact to remember: cut only through the top layers, the bottom is the foundation for the project. Slip your scissors under the top layers at the open end of the project. I cut between the stitching lines with my sharp Gingher scissors. After cutting all the way across to the end of the stitching line,

cut clips at 1" intervals. These clips make for full and fluffy fur.

*   There are new tools available that can be slipped into the area between the stitching lines, so the cutting can be made with a rotary cutter. When you use this tool and a rotary cutter, work with only light weight fabrics, such as a rayon challis. It is imperative that you are proficient with a rotary cutter or you could slip and ruin the project. I've only made projects with cottons.

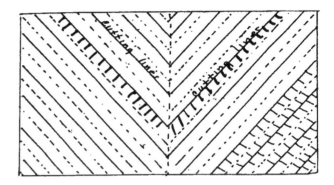

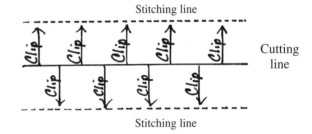

Stitching line · · · · · · · Cutting line · · · · · · · Stitching line

*   I suggest finishing the seam edges of your project by using a serger, stay stitching or zigzagging, when you finish clipping.
*   To "**fluff your fur**" wash the project in your washing machine. The agitation loosens up the threads on the cut and clip lines.
*   Dry in the clothes dryer and be prepared for a wonderful surprise. Not only the shading of the fabrics when they fluff, but the huge lint ball you will find in your dryer. Since the lint ball is all threads, it can be saved to make "Confetti Fabric" see page 87.

My winter Coat

My favorite "fabrique fur" project is my calf length coat. It has served as my every day winter coat for a number of years and I never tire of wearing it. It is very heavy and would only work in colder climates. Since I live in Nebraska, it is perfect. It was made from a KWIK SEW pattern with sleek, straight, simple lines.

Jenny's Winter Coat

Page 54 for color picture.

The foundation fabric for my coat is"trigger", a poly-cotton poplin that's been on the market for years. The top fabric is 6 oz. denim.

What luck I had on the sandwich fabrics. ****I found 60" 100% cotton sport weight cotton for $2.98 a yard. This was like finding a gold mine because this project took a lot of fabric for a full length coat and I was buying six times the yardage needed. Finding the 60" cotton in an array of colors was perfect. I used four different colors for the sandwich fabrics.

The stitching lines were marked 1" apart. Couching designer threads and yarns as I sewed, gave sparkle to the coat.

The following sketch gives you the directions for marking the stitching lines. For this project you need a 24" quilting ruler and marking pen or pencil. I marked, stitched and slashed each pattern section separately: then serged the edges and sewed the sections together following the pattern instructions.

This coat does not need a lining. Bias binding was used to finish the outside edge.

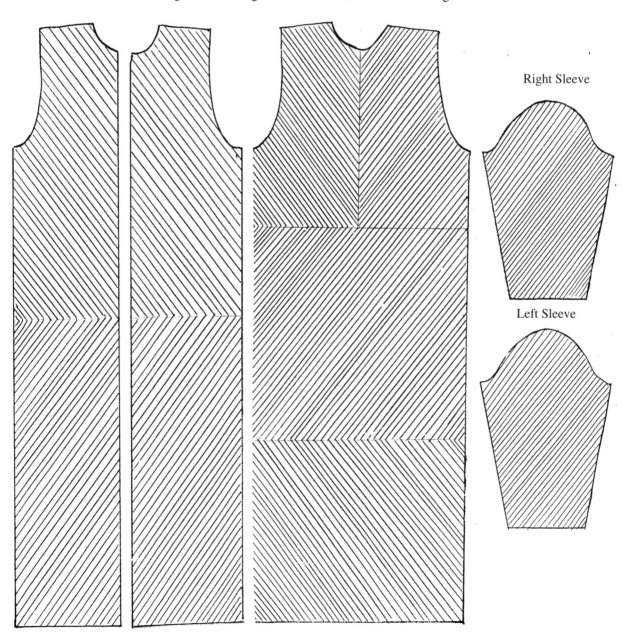

Right Sleeve

Left Sleeve

Fabrique Fur Jacket

Page 54 for color picture.

This awesome jacket is made on a sweatshirt base. The size is determined by the sweatshirt size. The design is achieved by layering fabrics, stitching and cutting. Purchase:

1 sweatshirt: select one with set in sleeves. The quality is not important as it is only used as the foundation and will be totally covered up. Preshrink if high cotton content.

Fabric: Ideas for top fabric are Bali prints, plaids, any large print, denim, chambray, you get a different look with each type fabric.

Top Fabric 2 1/2 yd. 100% cotton

Coordinating fabrics - 2 1/2 yd. each; solids or tone on tone prints. I suggest you have at least two inside layers, my jacket has five.

Preshrink all fabrics.

Purchased knit collar (if you can not find knit collars, I carry a large variety of colors in stock. See retail order information at the end of the book.

Separating zipper - measure your jacket front opening.

3/4" Bias tape maker

Thread to match top fabric and color of sweatshirt

Optional:

designer threads or yarns 60-70 total yards.

1 spool sulky metallic or sliver thread

.004 nylon thread

Follow the basic information on making a sweatshirt foundation jacket found on page 31.

A. Fabric or paper pattern

Lay your cut open sweatshirt on a large flat surface.

Sleeves

Lay pattern tracing material over sleeve, pin in several places. Use your fingers to feel the outline of the sleeve edges and sleeve armhole seam. You are feeling for the stitched seams on the sweatshirt. **Do not cut the sleeves out of the sweatshirt.** Mark pattern material with pen. Cut pattern 1/2" larger all the way around.

Back and fronts

Follow the same procedure as for the sleeve. For both front and back feel with your fingers for the area right below the neck ribbing. There is a little ditch so it is easy to find. The pattern for fronts and back may vary a little.

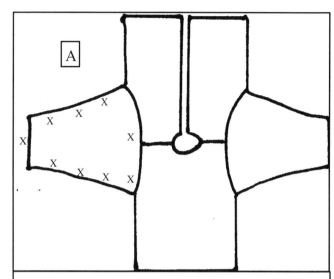

XXXX-Feel thru the pattern material for the edges marked with the X. Mark on the pattern. Do the same for the back and fronts.

B. Fabric Lay Out

Unfold each fabric to a single layer. Stack the fabrics, one of top of the other in an order that pleases you with the main fabric on the top.

Line up selvage edges along one side. They may not match exactly on both selvages as fabrics differ in width.

Use the fabric or paper pattern to cut out through all layers at once the fabrics as illustrated .

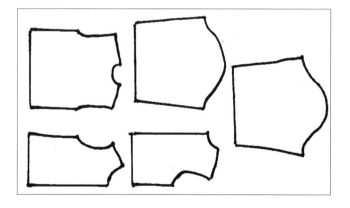

C. Front

Use a marking pen or pencil that can easily be seen and a 24" quilt ruler to mark your first drawing line on a 45° angle at the bottom edge of jacket front. See arrow for starting point. Mark all other lines 1" apart.

D. Back

Find center back and mark with straight pins. Measure down approximately 17" from top back as illustrated. For reference only mark the 17" line across with of jacket back with straight pins.

Mark the two lines (X) that meet in a V at the bottom of the top section. Let the first line be your guide to mark the other lines in the top sections 1" apart. Next mark the bottom section of jacket back. Now remove the straight pins.

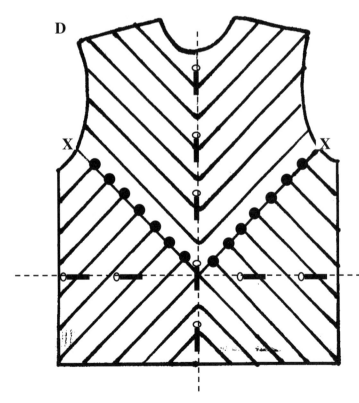

E. Sleeve

Mark sleeves as illustrated.

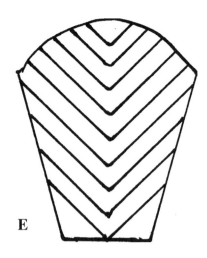

E

F. Placement of marked sections on sweatshirt

Apply one section at a time to sweatshirt working on a flat surface. Very carefully butt the raw neck edges on front and back to just below neck ribbing of sweatshirt. Pin well. Position sleeves. Butt shoulder seams of fronts and back. Pin all section well, making sure all is smooth and straight.

Sewing Lines

The marked lines are your sewing lines and they can be stitched two different ways.

- Stitch each line with coordinating thread to match top fabric.
- Couch designer threads as you stitch the lines. If you apply designer yarns and threads to the back section, where the small dot appears on the back top section , use a utility needle with a large eye and pull the yarn or thread to the underside and tie.

Stitch each sewing line in the same order you were asked to draw the lines. Remember to leave open the outside edge.

Cut strips of bias 1 1/4" wide. You need enough to cover raw edges between each fur section. Use a bias tape maker to fold the bias. Machine stitch in place.

Cutting and Clipping See page 47 for this information.
"Fluffing the Fur" see page 47 for this information.
To finish the jacket see page 33 for complete informa-

Summer Sand Vest

Color picture on page 54.

This vest is one of my favorites. I'm sure it's the beautiful hand painted fabrics from Micky Lawler of Skydyes. There was a big problem in making this vest, I barely had enough fabric. I normally purchase more than I need but this one time I didn't. I had to scrimp, it worked, but barely.

The basic design is very simple. Strips of fabric were cut 2" wide; then strip-pieced on each section with prairie points inserted in the seams as illustrated in the drawing.

Fabric

1 1/2 yd. fabric. This is for a Medium Size Vest.
For larger or longer vest, purchase extra fabric.

Steps to Follow

- Cut pattern pieces out of foundation fabric. The back pattern needs to be modified for this vest as illustrated in drawing B. See page 20 on modifying patterns. With a quilt ruler, accurately draw lines on the foundation as illustrated at A & B. If the strips of fabric are cut 2" wide, then the lines on the foundation must be 1 3/8" apart. This allows for turn room. Draw matching sections the same width. Please remember when marking your foundation, you may need more strips of fabric than what is sketched. Each pattern will be different. The sketch is for illustration purposes only.

- Count the number of strips your vest will need, then cut these 2" wide.

- Prairie Points: cut approximately 150 2/1/2" squares. If you have 8 different fabrics you will need 19 squares per fabric.

- **A. Front**: Allowing 1/4" seam allowance, strip piece the sections in the order suggested at (A). I suggest you finish lower sections then start with the top sections. If you stitch in this order you will be able to enclose all raw edges and easily insert the prairie points into the correct seam. Start piecing along the side on each section marked with a star.

- **B. Back**: On the lower back section start with the center strip of fabric and work your way out, this will make the piecing process much easier. You will see what I mean.

- Piece the upper back sections separately; then join at center back using 5/8"seam allowance as illustrated at **C**. Stitch top section to bottom, stitching each side separately into the dot. This is a set in point.

- **Embellishment**: I did not machine quilt my vest because I was short on time when it was made. To machine quilt, lift up the prairie points to get around them. I recommend stipple quilting. I couched a line of designer thread down each color line. To apply the cluster of beads on each prairie point, see on page 96.

- **Lining**: Place finished right sides of front and back sections to right side of lining fabric. Cut out lining. Stitch lining and vest together at shoulder and side seams. Press open seams. Place wrong sides together and baste the outside edges.

- Press well.

- Apply either plan bias binding or multi-colored binding found on page 115.

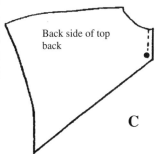

Back side of top back

C

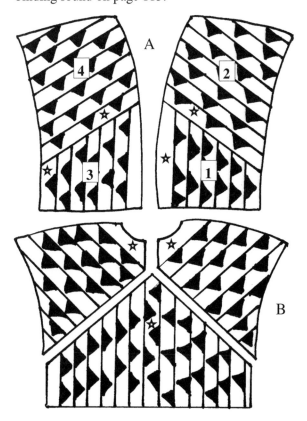

A

B

"Pick Up Sticks"

Color Picture on page 54.

This jacket is made from a black and white check fabric with strips of primary colors woven over the check to create a plaid.

The "pickup sticks" can be made two different ways. The strips of fabric for the plaid can be raw or have finished edges. On my jacket the edges are raw, the more it frays, the better. For finished edges, use a bias tape maker.

Fabric

Jacket: amount on pattern, plus 1/2 yard for bias binding. If you decide to use this design idea; I suggest you purchase fabric with no smaller than 1/2" nor larger than 1" squares. Cut main jacket pattern out of your selected fabric.

6 primary colors, tone on tone type fabrics, 1/2 yd. each. My colors were red, hot pink, purple, royal, yellow and lime green)

Set fabric colors: see page 26.

Foundation Fabric: see page 23.

Preshrink Fabrics: see page 26.

Fronts, back & sleeves of jacket: cut out of the check and foundation fabric.

Colored strips of fabric for plaid design

If the edge of the strips are to be finished, add 1/2" to allow for turn when using a bias tape maker. If the edge of the strips are to be raw, cut 1/2" wide strips.

Main body of jacket:

Cut 8, 1/2" x 45" strips of fabric for each color, for the body of jacket, sleeves & collar. You will have to see if you have enough strips cut.

When using a checkered fabric, follow the check design, leaving 2-3" between the strips. I wove the fabrics, pinned and then stitched down the center of each 1/2" strip with a double needle using black thread. For finished edges; stitch along each edge.

Back Yoke:

Cut 2, 1" x 45" strips of each color fabric.

Draw the yoke, using a black magic marker and a quilt ruler on the foundation fabric. Note that the yoke is cut at an odd angle. Cut out the yoke foundation. Use the 1" wide strips of fabric to weave on the yoke foundation as illustrated at **B**. The strips were used for both the woof and the warf in the weaving process. To achieve the same color design as in the picture on page 54, start with the same color on the horizontal as well as the vertical. By doing this you will get this off set color design. Mix colors as you desire. When finished, position on the jacket back section and stitch in place, leaving the edges raw.

Collar

If your pattern includes a collar, this is a good area for pin weaving. I used 1/8" narrow black ribbon, then wove the 1/2" strips.

Finishing

Finish jacket as per your pattern instructions, or bound the outside edge of the jacket with bias made from the checkered fabric or use multi-colored bias on page 115.

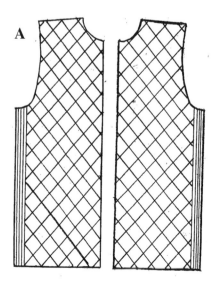

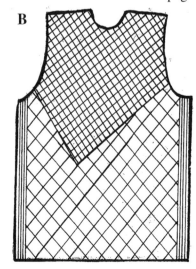

A Vest for all Seasons

Sands of Time Yellow

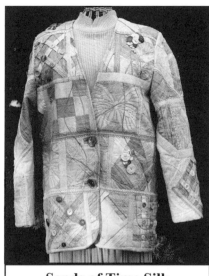

Sands of Time Silk

Fabric Flowers & Friends

Nomad

Button Bouquet

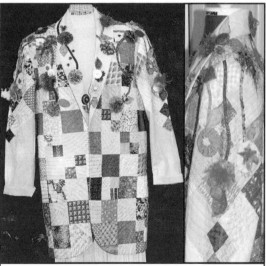

Patchy Patch Jacket

Patchy Patch Sweatshirt Jacket

Emerald Isle

Leather and Lace

Glitzy Chicken

Eye of the Tiger

Fabric Fur Coat and Jacket

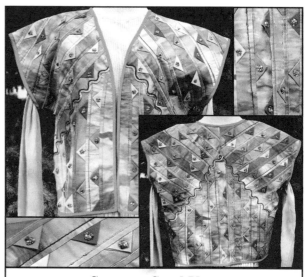

Summer Sand Vest

Arabesque the Vest

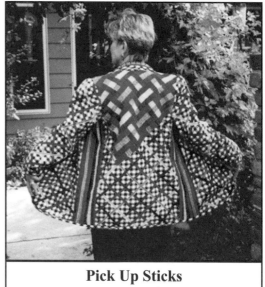

Pick Up Sticks

Patchy Patch Garden Jacket

Color picture on page 53.

Pattern
Purchase a jacket pattern with or without a lapel.

Fabric
Your jacket fabric will serve as the design base and lining. My fabric is 6 oz light blue chambray. This fabric was selected with care, because the jacket is not lined and it shows. It's also the lower part of the sleeves and lapel. Cut out the jacket fronts, back and sleeves.

Cut 150 assorted 3 1/2" squares of fabric. This jacket is a planned scrap design using many different fabrics. Many of the fabrics were from fabric club samples

This is the same design idea as my pattern, Patchy Patch Garden Sweatshirt Jacket. I wanted to do something a little different than the sweatshirt jacket so I covered the fronts and back with patches, but covered only the upper portion of the sleeves.

For variation, I made 4-Patch Squares to take the place of the 3 1/2 sqs. in several places.

Old coat buttons were used to embellish.

Purchase
Jacket Pattern
Fabric for jacket, see back of pattern.
Fabric Samples - if you have a large stash of 6" squares from a fabric club, they work well for this project.
Scraps of fabrics that work together
     or 1/4 yd. of 6-8 fabrics
3/4 yd. green for stems and leaves. For visual
     interest, use more than one green.
Flower color scraps for yoyo's
Large buttons. Old coat buttons are wonderful.
Designer threads or yarns for flower centers and
     flowers.
3/8" rayon ribbon for flowers.
Small buttons and seed beads for flower centers.

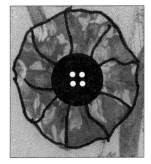
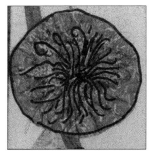

4-Patch Variation

To add design interest on this jacket, change some of the 3 1/2" squares into simple 4-Patch blocks. If you're using true 6" fabric samples; you can cut the 3 1/2" squares for the planned scrap patches and the 2" x 4" strips for the 4-patch. See illustration below.

If your color scheme is two colors, you need to cut 30- 2" x 4" strips of each color, get a good combination of fabrics, this is for 30 pairs.

If using purchased yardage you will need to cut 2" wide strips.

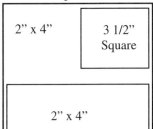

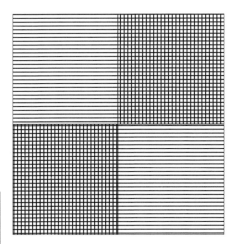

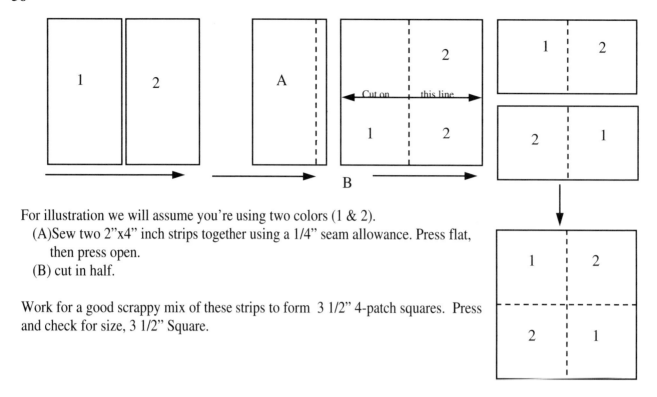

For illustration we will assume you're using two colors (1 & 2).
  (A) Sew two 2"x4" inch strips together using a 1/4" seam allowance. Press flat, then press open.
  (B) cut in half.

Work for a good scrappy mix of these strips to form 3 1/2" 4-patch squares. Press and check for size, 3 1/2" Square.

Front and Back Fabric Layout Diagrams

Use the following charts to design your jacket fronts and back. Where there is an + in the square, place a 4-patch square. Chart (C) is for use with two fabrics, Chart (D) is for a mix. If you can, lay out jacket on a design wall.

C

D

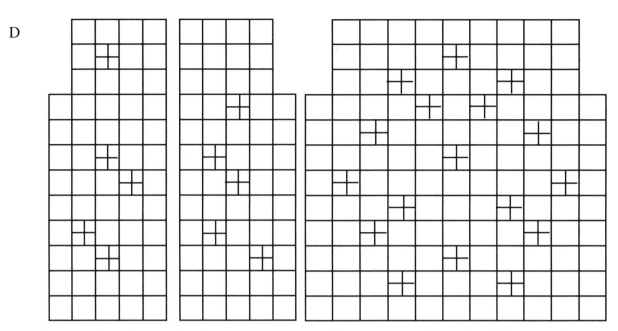

When you have have a pleasing arrangement, sew the squares together using 1/4" seam allowances. Press sections well. To assist with getting the squares to your machine, see my hint at the top of page 12 under another use for padded quilter's board.

Check to see if the pieced sections are big enough for your pattern, if not add more squares. Lay front and back onto pieced sections. If necessary; add squares at side seams. Use the guide at (E). Your pattern will not fit exactly as illustrated, this is only an example. Be very careful to work for a good match at center front and side seams.

When you are completely sure, then cut out the fronts and back using cut fabric pieces as pattern. Pin or stitch baste these sections together, see basting page 32.

Finish the jacket as per your pattern instructions.

E

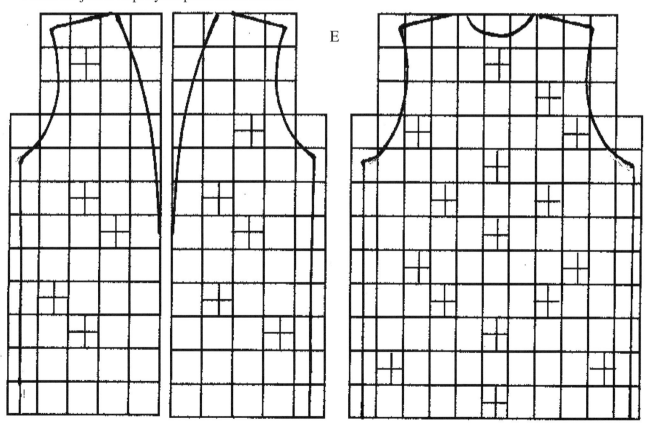

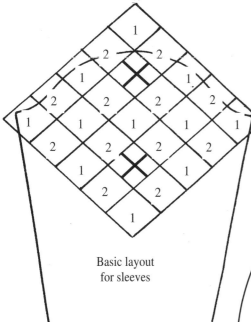

Basic layout
for sleeves

Fabric Yo-Yos and Yarn Flowers and Centers

This information can be found on page 100.

Circle templates for large and small
yo-yos. Cut out circles, turned under
1/4" and hand stitch and gather tight
and secure. Use your fingers to shape.

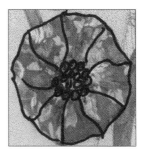

Arabesque the vest

Color Picture on page 54

Arabesque was designed for a retreat at my home several years ago. It is a beautiful vest, with several different sections, each with a different piecing or quilting technique. "Fussy Cutting" was used. This technique adds so much to the vest.

Background Fabric

This vest is divided into different sections, most of the fabrics are used in each section. The first selection is the background fabric. Anyone who has ever taken a class from me or heard my lectures will know that I consider the background fabric a very important part of my fabric selection. For "Arabesque" I selected the Black/Gold Stars from Spiegel. I have used it in many of my projects; it is a great piece of fabric. Select your background fabric with care, it can make or break your project.

Fussy Cutting

You will be doing some wonderful fussy cutting. I selected three different fabrics for this. I thought they were all so pretty, I couldn't decide which one to use. If you select only one fabric, it will do just find. See page 63 for picture examples of fabric for fussy cutting.

My fabric color families included fuchsia, purple, royal blue, turquoise, plus splashes of yellow and other colors.

Coordinating Fabrics

These are the fabrics that complement your fussy cut fabric and background fabric. My favorites are tone on tone, watercolor, Bali type fabric with many shades of one color. Today the selections are fabulous for this type of project. Please do not select fabrics that have a lot of different colors, they will fight your fussy cut fabrics and you may not like the end result. Give yourself a good selection, you will want to audition different fabrics in your project.

Design Wall

It's very important that you use a design wall for this project. See page 12 for details.

Fabric requirements

Background & Binding Fabric - 1 1/2 yards of 45" fabric
3/4 yd. 1-2 different fussy cutting fabric (see page 62)
Coordinating fabrics - 1/3 yd. of 8+ fabrics
6" squares - you are going to need a lot of different fabrics for the basic design of this vest. If you are part of a fabric club - go through the squares and pick out squares that will coordinate with the above. Don't choose fabrics with too many light colors as they tend to stick out in a design, choose fabrics that will blend well when viewed at a distance. If you do not belong to a fabric club, bring a large selection of fabrics that blend.
Lining - check your pattern for amount
Batting - Lt. Weight or foundation fabric
Pattern Tracing Fabric - 2 yards.
1 yd. Wonder Under
Several cards designer threads (50 yards)
2 spools metallic thread
2 Spools Rayon thread to coordinate with your fabrics.
1 1/4 yd - 3/4" wide decorative ribbon, ornate buttons, etc.
Sewing thread to match fabrics
.004 Nylon thread
9" piece of Non-Roll Elastic
3.0 or 4.0 twin machine needle
1 sheet **clear** template
45° Triangle Ruler
60° Triange Ruler

Vest - Select the vest pattern of your choice resembling this illustration.

Pattern Fitting

Trace your tissue pattern onto the pattern tracing material, including all markings. Cut traced pattern out and pin at side seam and shoulder to check for fit and length.

Pattern Modification

After you have a good fit with the foundation fabric, trace onto pattern tracing material. Use your quilt ruler and a pencil to divide the correctly fitted pattern front into divisions illustrated. See pages 20 and 21 for complete information.

Mark grain lines on all sections.

Use measurements given within each section to help determine correct section size.

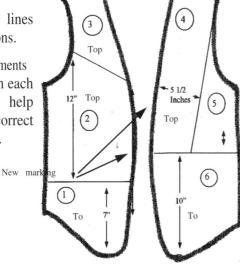

Making Pattern Pieces from the new Sections

Use the other half of your tracing material to make individual patterns for each of the sections. DO NOT CUT APART YOUR MARKED MAIN PATTERN SECTIONS. Mark the seam allowance already on your pattern on each section, add 1/4" seam allowance as you trace each new pattern section. See top of page 21. This is added only on your new marking line, not on the original pattern section. Mark each section so that you know it's the top, not reverse side.

DOUBLE CHECK - Double Check to make sure each section is correct.

Now take that "ugly fabric" from the back of the closet and cut out Fabric Foundation Pattern sections 1-6 , making note of grainlne of fabric. Cut 1back section.

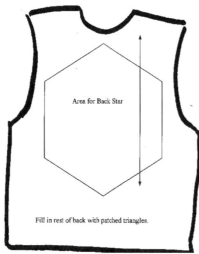

The following piecing arrangement is for the patched back vest section. If you Fussy Cut any of your triangles place them in area of ***

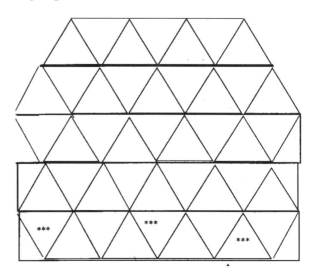

Triangle Template

The 45° template to cut your assortment of fabrics is on page 69. Use your Fussy Cut Fabric to cut 2 or 3 triangles in this manner.

Unless stated differently, 1/4" seam allowance will be used for the piecing of all sections.

Section 1

Cut 8 different fabrics into 3" x 10" Strips.
Sew them together on long edge until they resemble the following.

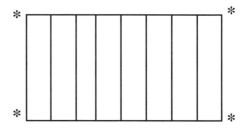

Place the sewn section in a sink of water; wring out excess water. Fold * corners together and fold again. Now twist fabric until it rolls up in a knot. Secure ends. Place fabric in warm place to dry. I use my food dehydrator. See page 84. If you dry in your clothes dryer, place in a knee high stocking, secure, then dry with a load of clothes. When it's dry, unwrap and lay flat as possible leaving wrinkles (that's why we did this in the first place). Iron fusible interfacing to the back of section.

Use pattern for section one to cut out. Baste section 1 to foundation.

Section 2

Cut 2 - 1" x 45" strips of background fabric
Cut 1 1/2" x 10" strips of 12 different fabrics. Divide these fabrics up into six different pairs. Sew together pairs along long edge. Press each section well. Cut these strips into 4 - 2 1/2" Squares.

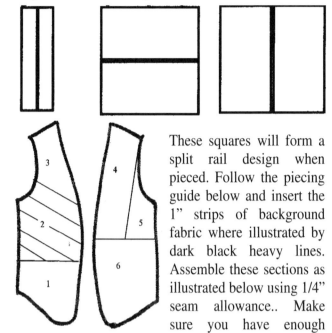

These squares will form a split rail design when pieced. Follow the piecing guide below and insert the 1" strips of background fabric where illustrated by dark black heavy lines. Assemble these sections as illustrated below using 1/4" seam allowance.. Make sure you have enough pieced to cover section 2. Before sewing the sections together, lay together to This section is cut on an angle as shown above. Use the pattern for section 2 and cut out. Fuse baste on foundation fabric.

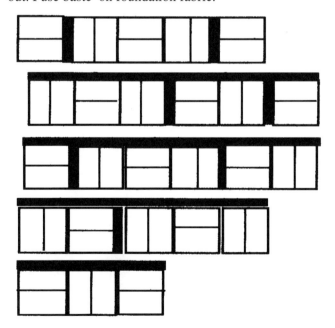

Section 3

Cut this section out of your background fabric using section 3 Fabric Foundation pattern. Fuse Baste.

Section 4

Cut 2 - 14" x 8" pieces of fabric, 1 out of bright fabric, 1 background fabric.
Quick Piece Right Triangle Squares. Lay your two fabrics together right sides together.
On wrong side. Draw the following. The squares are 2 3/4" squares

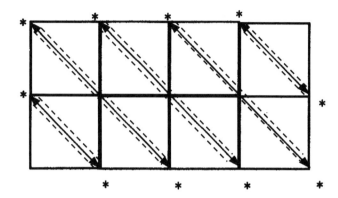

Draw a diagonal line through each square from point to point as illustrated. Pin baste. Using a 1/4" seam allowance, sew on either side of the drawn lines. * Press entire section when finished stitching and then cut squares apart on drawn lines.

Next cut on drawn line each square into two sections. Open and you have one right triangle square. Press.

Arrange the Right Triangle Squares into Pinwheel blocks as illustrated

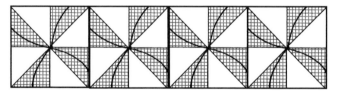

Stitch the four block together, end to end. Press well. Cut 1 - 2" x 18" piece of background fabric and stitch along one long edge. Press well.

Section 5

Layer foundation fabric with background fabric. Cut section five noting top.

Section 6

Cut fabric samples for each template to help you remember their placement.

1._____ 2._____

3._____ 4._____

5._____ 6._____

7._____

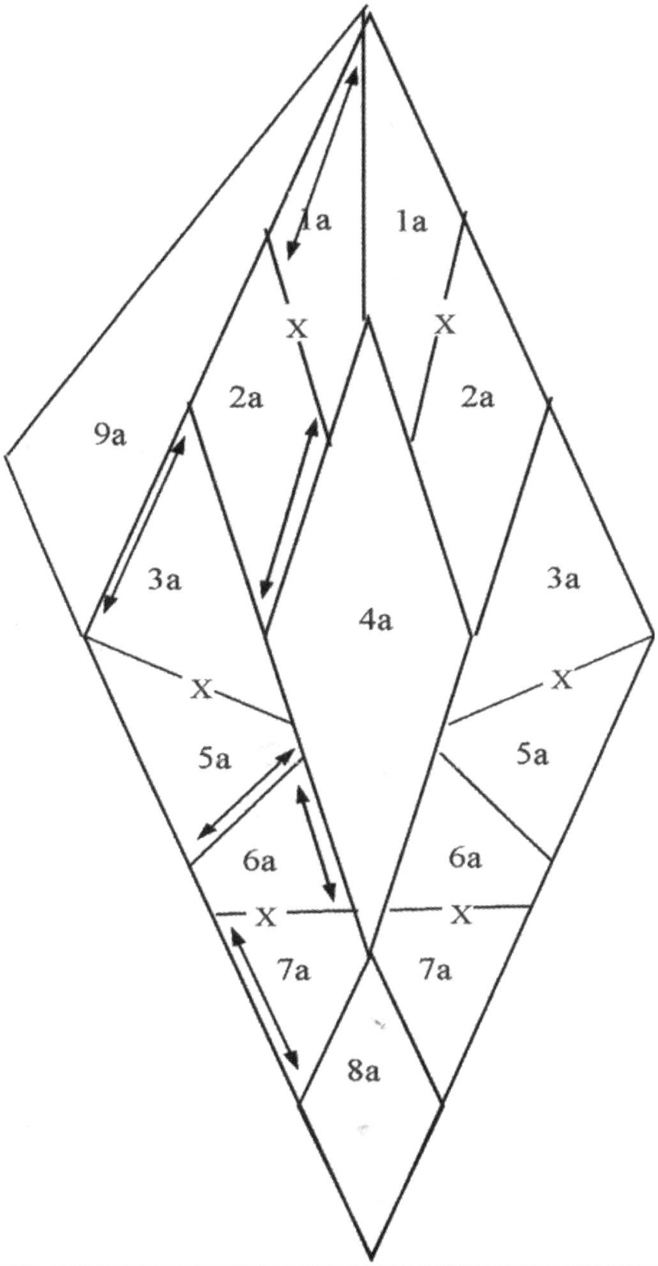

Placement of fabrics in Block. Cut snips of your coordinating fabric and lay them on the sketch of star point. You will need to do this for 1, 2, 3, 5, 6, and 7. In the original vest #9a is cut from background fabric .

Front Star Section. For this section we will piece 3 points from an 8 Point Star.

The templates for this star are on page 67. Use clear template plastic. It's important that you can see the design of your fabric. Mark all notations on templates.

Quick Piece Combinations

Make 3 star sections and quick piece combinations of templates 1a & 2a , 3a & 5a as well as 6a & 7a. Each template will be illustrated on star but the templates on pages 67 68 are printed as a combination. This allows for quick piecing of these sections.

Cut: (double check these measurements)
template 1a - 2 1/4" wide x 31"
template 2a - 1 3/4" wide x 31"
template 3a - 2 1/2" wide x 18"
template 5a - 2 1/4" wide x 18"
template 6a   2" wide x 15"
template 7a -2 1/2" wide 15"

Strip piece fabrics for these sections using 1/4" seam allowance, press. Lay the template, matching the dotted line on template to the seam on the fabric and cut both sections at once. For each section you will need 3 cut in one direction and 3 cut in the opposite direction, as illustrated to the right.

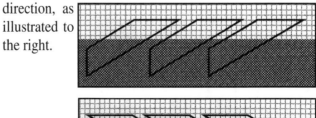

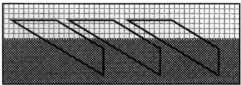

Fussy Cutting

This is a simple illustration of fussy cutting. Place your template over a design. What you see inside the seam allowance is what you'll see in the finished block. Fussy Cutting Template 4a and 8a.

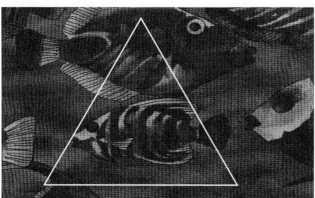

I enjoy surprises in my work and will often have a fish, butterfly or a bug moving through my project. Leaf motif's are one of my favorites for fussy cutting.

Piecing Assembly for 8 point star

A good portion of this block is a straight set but there are two set in points, each noted with a black dot. These take patience but can be achieved with good results. When piecing stars, use lots of pins to pin through all intersecting points. After completing each section, use your 45 degree triangle to straighten each section. If using optional section 9a, add after each section is trimmed.

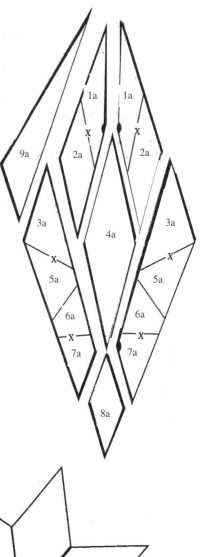

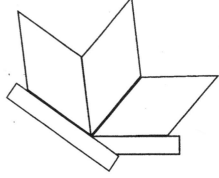

Next stitch three star points together; carefully pin so design matches across. To the bottom edges add 3" wide strips of fabric to fill in the corner. The width of these strips could vary from pattern to pattern.

To stitch star sections to Section 5, turn & press under 1/4" seam allowance on outside edge of star. Use .004 nylon thread (so your stitches won't show) to stitch the star in place.

Section 7- Back *Star*

See next page.

This is a Six point Star. The design shown is for one of the 6 points of a 60° triangle.

Templates for this star can be found on page 68.

Trace the templates using clear template plastic. It's important that you can see thru the plastic so to see the design of your fabric.

Cut fabric samples for each template to help you remember your fabric placement and to help design your star.You will need to do this for 2b, 3b, 4b, 5b and 6b. In the original vest # 4 is cut from Background fabric as well as optional template # 9b.

Fussy Cut Template 1b, 7b and 8b. See illustration on previous page.

1._____ 2._____

3._____ 4._____

5._____ 6._____

7._____

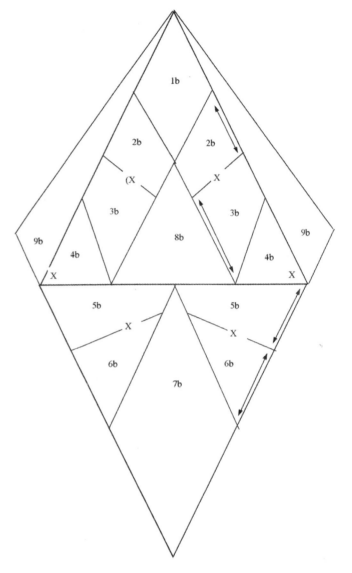

Quick piece combinations of template 2 & 3, as well as template 5 & 6. Each template is illustrated on star drawing but the templates on page 67 are printed as a combination. This allows for quick piecing of these sections.

Cut strips of fabric as follows for 6 star points

2b cut 2 1/4" wide x 31"

3b cut 2 /2" wide x 31"

5b cut 1 3/4" x 40"

6b cut 2" wide x 40"

After cutting these strips the width needed, sew 2 & 3 and 5 & 6 together with 1/4" seam allowance. Press seam to one side. Lay your combined template with correct section # to fabric # and (X) line along seam line. Mark and cut out carefully. For each section you will need 6 cut in one direction and 6 cut in the opposite direction. See illustration on next page.

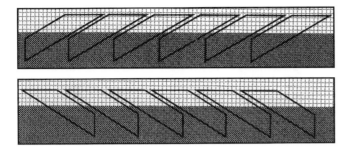

Piecing Assembly for each Diamond

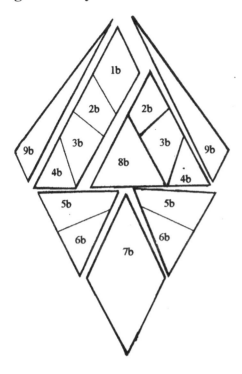

Use .004 nylon thread to stitch star in place.

Machine Quilted - I stipple quilted the star area, except for the outside points. On these points I did random twin needle machine quilting from point to point.

After the star was applied and quilted, I couched Designer Thread on the patch section outside the star.

After completing each section, use your 60 degree ruler to straighten up each section. If using Optional Section 9b, add it after each section is trimmed. Stitch the six star sections together, being careful to pin and match at each seam. When complete press well, but carefully, do not push the star out of shape.

Vest Back

Assemble the patch portion of the back of the vest. Take the Fabric Foundation piece for back and position over patch area. Press the two together, making sure everything is flat. Fuse baste. Cut batting if using for back and Fuse baste in place. Use a twin needle and metallic thread, then random machine quilt over this area.

Apply large Star

Press under 1/4" on all outside edges of star. Position on back with one of the points about 2" below top center back. Make sure the star is very flat, pin baste.

Let the Embellishing Begin

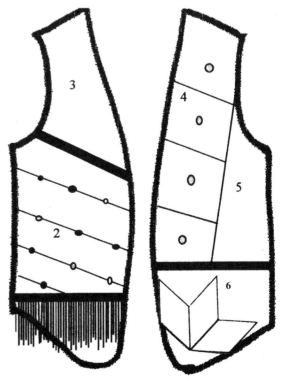

Section 1

Use a twin needle and various colors of Sulky Rayon thread to random machine quilt over this area. Fringe

Take a 4" x 6" piece of heavy cardboard and use to wrap various designer threads and Sulky metallic threads. Wrap 4-5 times. Use a large utility hand needle with large eye and string to slip through one end of loops and tie with a knot. Leave a tail. Cut the other end and you have a small tassel. Make at least 20 of these. They will be stitched at the top edge of section l.

Section 2

Use a twin needle to do machine quilting on this area. Couch designer threads over this area. Embellish at random points with large beads or buttons.

Section 3

Use a twin needle to do curvy stitching as illustrated.

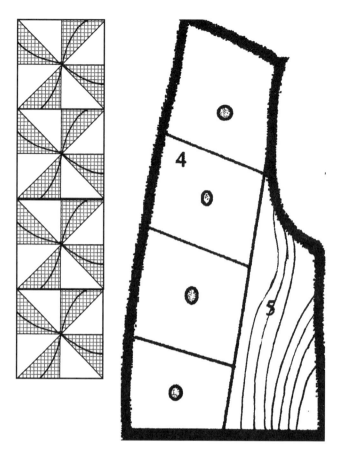

Next stitch 3/4" wide decorator ribbon to enclose sections of 1 & 2 and 2 & 3 as illustrated on page 54.

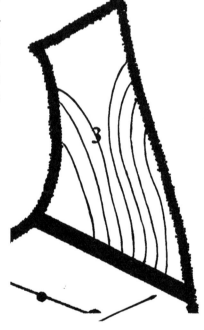

Section 5

Use a twin needle and Sulky Metallic thread to stitch curvy lines as illustrated.

Section 6

On the background random machine quilt. Stitch 3/4" decorator ribbon between sections 5 and 6.

On the outside edge of the star section, press under 1/4". This star section is to be positioned at the bottom corner of vest as illustrated. Use .004 nylon thread & top stitch from left to right two of the star sections. Do not stitch down 3rd right point. This will be done later as it may lap over side seam onto back section.

Section 4

Place assembled Pinwheel section along front edge. Adjust to fit. Stitch section 4 to Section 5. Stipple quilt the background fabric on 4 and 5 using Sulky's Sliver. Use a twin needle and Sulky Metallic Thread to do a swirl movement like a Pinwheel for each colored section. In the center of each Pinwheel block place a decorative button or bead. On section 5 use a twin needle and Sulky Metallic thread to stitch curvy lines as illustrated

Back Section

Use a twin needle and random machine quilt the patch part of the back section. Couch designer threads if desired. Press under 1/4" seam allowance around the outside edge of the six point star. Position on back section and stitch around edge with .004 nylon thread to hide stitches. Machine quilt using a twin needle as illustrated below.

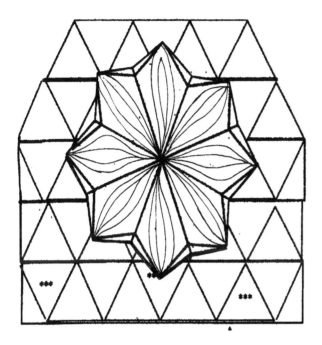

Charm & Buttons

I did not use charms on my jacket but they would be great placed in special little areas. Clusters of buttons might be very attractive as well. Use your imagination, what else would spruce up your already wonderful jacket.

Lining

The lining can be embellished with fabric paint. Take a 2" sq. piece of compressed sponge (available at craft stores) and cut it into any shape you like. I suggest you make a sample, play around on a small piece of lining fabric before you do this on actual lining. You could also use stencils to add design or freehand paint, if you are a painter.

Assembling Front and Back Sections

Use the finished fronts and back as your pattern. Cut out your lining a 1/2" larger around the outside edge of your finished fronts and back. **Do not add** extra 1/2" to shoulder or side seams.

Embellish, if you desire.

Stitch both lining and vest fronts and back together at shoulders and side seams. Press Open. At this time lay the third point of front star down onto the back of the vest. Finish top stitching that portion of the star.

Machine quilt the front star. Random swirl machine quilt the background fabric area of star, using a twin needle with metallic thread machine quilt in a curved design to give the points sparkle.

With wrong sides together, place raw edges of vest and lining. Work to fit, allowing extra 1/2 inch to lap over edge. After all fits as it should, baste edges together and trim away excess fabric.

Bias Binding

Measure the outside edge of vest plus arm holes. Cut this amount of 2 1/4" wide bias out of your background fabric. Apply as you would to a quilt edge, bound the outside edge of vest. You could also use Multi-Colored Bias as on page 115.

68

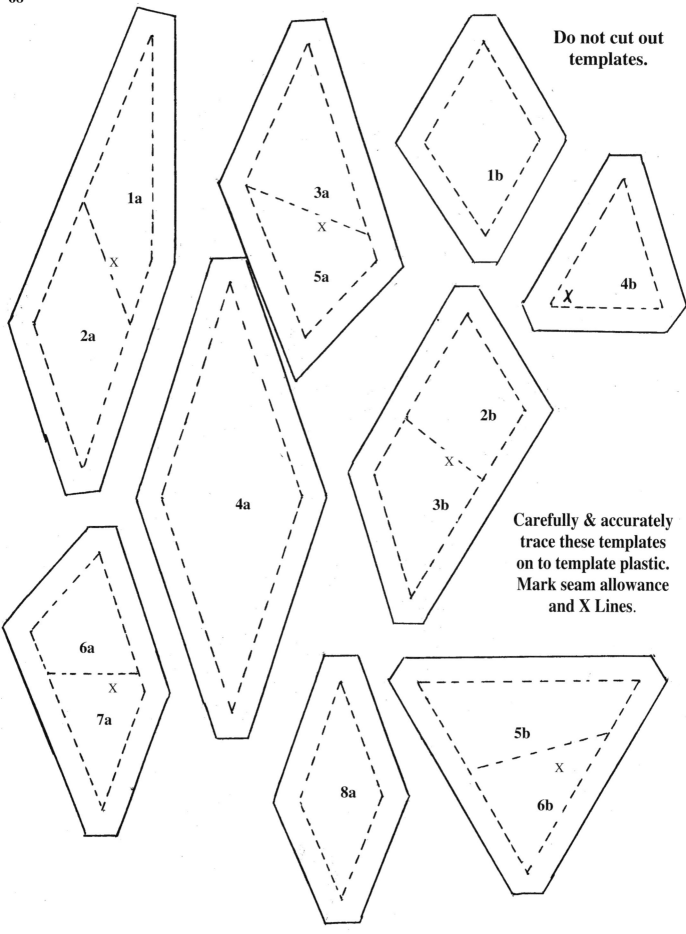

Do not cut out
templates.

1a

3a

X

5a

1b

4b

X

2a

X

2b

X

3b

4a

Carefully & accurately
trace these templates
on to template plastic.
Mark seam allowance
and X Lines.

6a

X

7a

8a

5b

X

6b

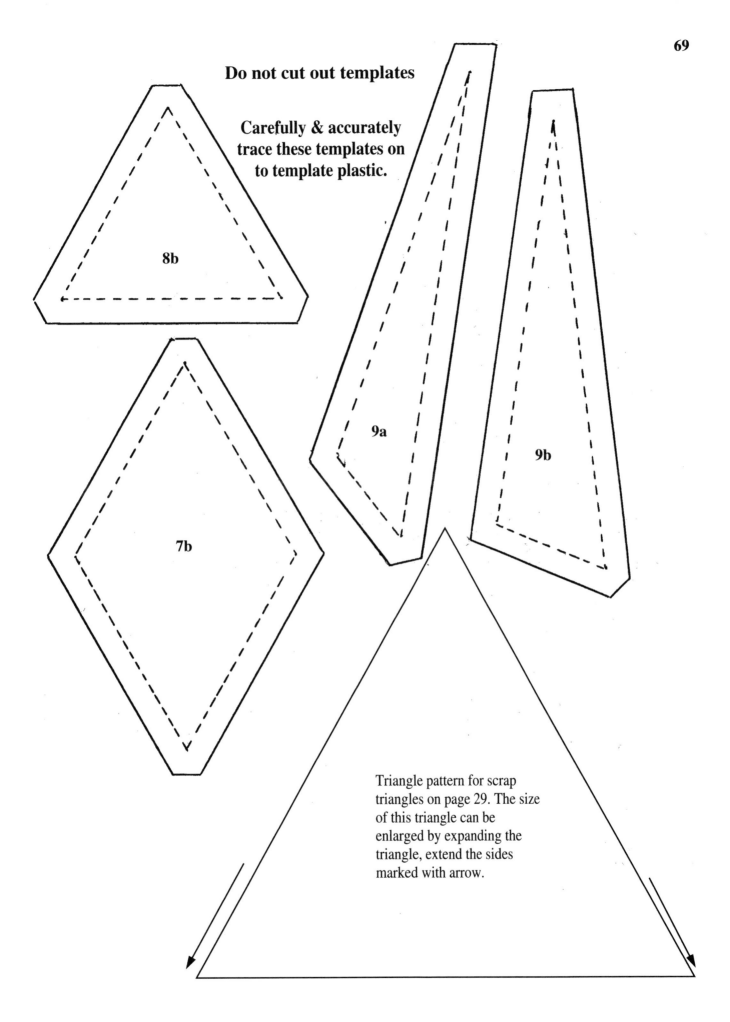

Do not cut out templates

Carefully & accurately trace these templates on to template plastic.

8b

7b

9a

9b

Triangle pattern for scrap triangles on page 29. The size of this triangle can be enlarged by expanding the triangle, extend the sides marked with arrow.

Sands of Time Jacket

Pictures on page 53

Jacket #1 is made from straight set blocks as illustrated on the next page. The original jacket was made from a collection of Cherrywood Fabrics, with the main fabric being a butter yellow.

The blocks on jacket #2 are off set as illustrated on the next page. The original is made from a collection of neutral silks–collected over many years. Both jackets are a composite of simple patch designs that can be embellished with twin needle machine quilting, designer threads and yarns, ribbons, trims and braids as well as buttons and pearls. Button bouquets are scattered over the jacket in a pleasing manner. Page 95.

Both jackets are made on a foundation fabric, no batting was used in the original. A light weight poplin was used for both the original jackets and I did not line either one. I omitted the lining, so the jackets would be cooler to wear. If you plan to line your jacket, use a medium weight fabric for the foundation. The other option for the foundation is to use any old fabric, something you want to hide. See page 23.

Wash, dry and press all fabrics ahead of time, see page 26 for complete information.

Select a jacket pattern without a lapel.

Fabrics: I suggest you use solid fabrics or those that read as solids; such as Bali prints, tone on tones or hand dyes for this project. Fabric for jacket #1 came from:

Hand Dyed Fabrics by Cherrywood Fabrics, Inc. see page 15 for complete information.

Color cards are available and the selection is unbelievable. I suggest you call or email and order a color card.

Purchase:

Main fabric - See the back of your pattern for the amount plus 1 1/2 yards.

This fabric will serve as your background fabric.

I suggest a fabric that blends with all your fabrics. My jacket is a butter yellow with the other fabrics being shades that suggest southwest.

Companion fabrics - 6-8 1/2 yard cuts of fabric

4 yd.

Wonder Under

Designer threads (50 yds) if you can not find these in your area, I carry a full line. Send swatches of your fabric and I will select a good combination for your project.

2 spools Metallic Thread

2 Spools Sulky Rayon thread that either matchs or complements your fabrics. Note the variegated threads.

Button Bouquets: Old mother of pearl buttons and others were used on my silk jacket. For the southwestern jacket I found buttons of various shapes and colors.

Sewing thread to match background fabric.

.004 Nylon thread

3.0 or 4.0 twin machine needle

Jacket Size: Make a muslin from your pattern for correct fit. This jacket is sewn with no side seams so it must fit before the blocks are applied to the foundation fabric. See page 28 for information on determining number and size of blocks to be used in this project.

Six different blocks will be made

1 - Pinwheel block   # 2 - Crazy Quilt Block
3- Shadow Box block # 4 - Crisscross - Straight
5 - Crisscross - Angle # 6 - 9 Patch

For visual purposes, the main jacket section will resemble a small quilt. There are no side seams on the jacket to allow for one continuous design. The jacket muslin that has been fit to your figure will serve as the pattern after the blocks are assembled and embellishments are complete.

Use 1/4" seam allowance to piece the blocks. The blocks are not sewn together. Instead, they will be lined up, probably with a narrow space between each block. Use fusible web to stabilize the blocks. I suggest you arrange the blocks as illustrated on the next page. Edge stitch around each of the blocks after they have been fused to the foundation.

Embellish now. First, machine quilting. I used a twin needle and the stitching was done in a random manner, see page 91 for ideas. After machine quilting, apply designer threads and yarns in a random manner.

The final touch is the addition of the connecting strips of fabric. For the silk jacket I used different neutral ribbons and trims. At times sewing narrow trim on wider ribbons. If using fabric strips, gauge the width these strips need to be for your jacket. To that width add at least 1/2" and use a bias tape maker for firm edges. Sew the vertical strips first and then the horizontal. Double check center front to make sure you have a horizontal match.

Beads and/or buttons are sewn at this time.

Jacket # 1

Layout for Yellow Cherrywood Jacket - Straight Set Jacket

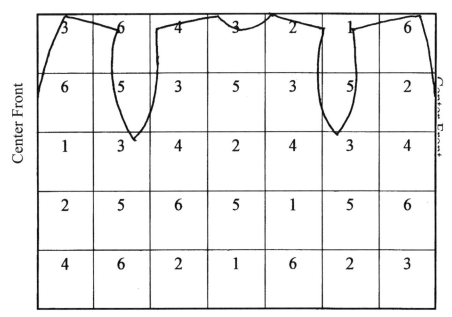

Block #	# of blocks to be made
Block 1	6
Block 2	8
Block 3	7
Block 4	7
Block 5	7
Block 6	8

Chart for straight set jacket.

This is the layout for jacket # 1. It is very important that the blocks along center front line up straight. This is a good place to use a quilt ruler.

The drawing is for illustration only. How jacket will fit on the pieced section, is not exact.

Jacket # 2

Layout for off-set blocks, the original is made of silk fabrics.

Block #	# of blocks t to be made
Block 1	8
Block 2	11
Block 3	9
Block 4	6
Block 5	8
Block 6	6

Chart for off-set jacket.

The layout for jacket #2 is off-set as illustrated. The chart includes blocks for the sleeves. It is very important that the blocks along center front are same distance from the bottom on both sides, see arrows, as this will meet in center front. Use a quilt ruler here.

The drawing is for illustration only. How your jacket fits on the pieced section could be different.

Determined the block size for this project, use accurate 1/4" graph paper to draw each of the six blocks in this project.

Block # 1 - Pinwheel Block

Plan to use all of your colors for the pin wheels. Multiply the number of blocks to be made by 4, then divide this number by the number of different fabrics you have. This will give you the number of right triangle squares to be made for each color.

Number of blocks _____ x 4 = _____ divided by _____ # of different fabrics = _____ number of right triangle squares to be made for each color.

Squares: the size of these squares will be the size of a finished pin wheel plus 7/8 inch. See outlined pinwheel section. Check your graph paper for this measurement. Make sure you are sure before you cut your fabric.

Size of Squares to cut will be _____ Number of blocks_____ x 2 = _____ number of background fabric squares.

Divide the number of background squares _____ by the # of different fabrics_____ x 2 = number of squares to be cut for each fabric.

To sew the right triangle squares: lay out all background fabric squares. On top lay the different colors. Piece as illustrated on page 30. After you quick piece the triangles, get a good mix and assemble the pinwheels as shown.

Block # 2- Crazy Quilt Block

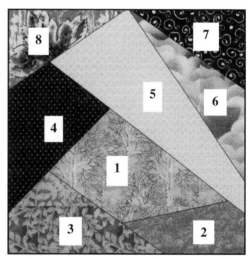

This is an easy and fun block to piece. For each crazy quilt block in this projects cut squares of background fabric the size each block was determined to be on page 72, second column. Draw this crazy quilt design onto the squares of fabric, then number each section as illustrated. This will be the order in which you sew sections of fabric to the squares.

Cut 1, 3" wide strip of fabric for each color including background fabric. Place the background fabric in each block and try to place in a different position for each block. Move the colors around and it will be hard to realize they all come from the same design.

After you have assemble all of your Crazy Quilt Blocks, trim edges to your block size and then baste stitch around each block to stabilize fabrics.

Block # 3 - Shadow Box Block

This is a simple block to make. Check the chart on the previous page for how many blocks need to be made. Draw this block on the 1/4" graph paper. From the graph paper, trace templates. Cut the center block from the back ground fabric. Work for a good mix of your other fabrics for the outside portions of the block.

Block # 4 - Crisscross Straight Block

You will need to cut _____squares of Background fabric.

To start, cut 2 - 1 3/4" wide strip of each color. With right sides together, stitch together each strip using 1/4" seam allowance. Leave ends open. Sew all strips, then turn each to outside using safety pin or ballpoint bodkin.

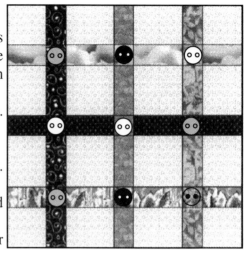

After all are turned, press well with seam allowance on underside. This should give you enough for both Crisscross Straight and Angle.

Crisscross Straight Blocks

You need 6 strips per block the length of your finished block. _____inches.

Number of strips per block 6 x _____# of blocks needed =_____# of Strips.

# of Strips needed_____divided by # of colors = cut strips per color _____.

Mark outside lines 1 3/4" from center line.

Use six different colors for each square. Get a good mix. Using the marked line as a guide, position the strips of fabric so that they are centered on the marked line. Pin in place. Pin edge of outside strips along outside lines. Make sure you weave the strips as you lay them on the fabric. This looks better.

Use nylon thread to stitch down in place.

Block # 5 - Crisscross Angle Block

Cut_____squares of Background fabric.

Measure the distance from corner to corner plus one inch. Cut two strips per block that length, work for a good mix. Do not repeat the same fabric on a block.

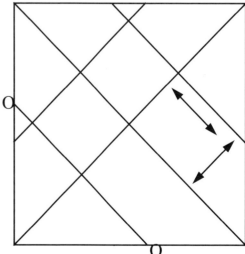

The distance between the center lines and the outside lines is 2". Mark lightly.

Check distance of outside lines (O) and add one inch. Cut the rest of strips into this length. Be sure and weave the strips as it will look better.

Stitch strips in place with nylon thread.

Embellishment

The silk jacket illustrated on page 53 was embellished with a button at each strip intersection.

Block # 6 - 9 Patch Block

Draft this block on your 1/4" graph paper. Be sure to add 1/4 seam allowance to templates. I did not quick piece as there were so few blocks to make and I wanted to use all different colors.

For each block, cut 4 background squares.

Cut five different colors.

Try to make each block with different fabric combinations.

Sleeves

Cut sleeves out of the background fabric and backing fabric. The silk jacket has three blocks on each sleeve, the yellow jacket has four. Decide which you like best. Secure blocks to sleeves the same way you did on the main jacket section.

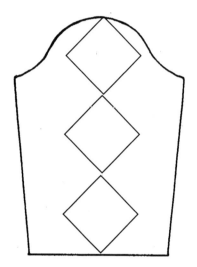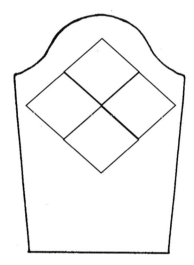

Finishing

When you are finished with the blocks and embellishing, sew the jacket together as per your pattern instructions. Cut the jacket facing from one of the main jacket fabrics. If you do not plan to line the jacket, remember to finish the outside edges of the facing.

Fairfield & Bernina Fashion Show Ensemble........

For those of you who are not familiar with these two shows, the Fairfield Fashion Show was started in 1977 by Donna Wilder of Fairfield Processing. After 23 years. Donna made a career change and Fairfield decided to drop the show. Quilts, Inc. in Houston and Bernina made the bold move to continue the show, thus the Bernina Fashion Show was born in 2001. Myself, and other designers, will be forever grateful to Karey Bresenhan and Bernina for their foresite to continue this venue for wearable designers to create works of art and for audiences around the world to enjoy.

The show is a success because of the many corporate sponsors, who either give or sell at a discount; notions, fabrics and patterns to the designers to be used in their design. The first several years after the selections list was revealed, "goodie box's" started to arrive from the many sponsors. I had no idea all this would happen the first year, so it was all the more fun each time the doorbell rang and a new package was at my front door. It was just like Christmas, with great surprises in the boxes.

Over time, I have received notion items, patterns and a little fabric but on the whole, I have paid for my garments. From the beginning I knew that the products I used in my garments had to be the perfect in my mind, even if I had to pay for them. I have no idea how much these garments have cost me and I do not want to. It would be scary! It has been worth every dollar I spend on fabrics, the right shoes, jewelry and accessories, because when my "baby" comes out on the runway and strolls to the music under the lights. Oh yeah.......what a rush!

1994 Fairfield Fashion Show - "Starlight Rhapsody"- Finale Garment in the show

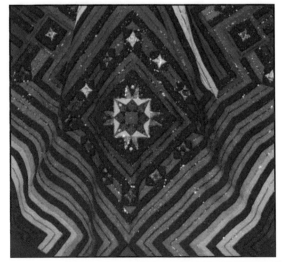
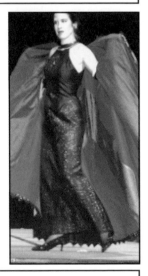

1995 Fairfield Fashion Show - "Joseph's Jubilation, Splendeur of Galaxias"

76

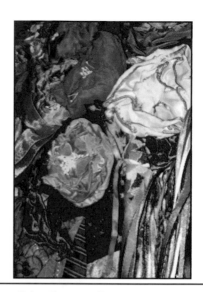

1997 20th Anniversary Fairfield Fashion Show - "Arabesque"

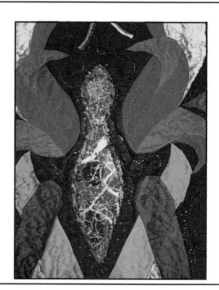

2001 Premier Bernina Fashion Show - "From Nebraska with Love"

2002 Bernina Fashion Show - "Diamonds are a Girl's Best Friend" - Viewers Choice Award

"Starlight Rhapsody" 1994 Fairfield Fashion Show

I dug deep into my files and found the paper work for "Starlight Rhapsody". I'm going to share what I wrote back in 1994. These are the random thoughts of a real "newbie".

- *"I started day dreaming about this garment the summer of 1993 when a friend encouraged me to try for the Fairfield Fashion Show. I felt my chances were slim; but the wheels started to turn long before I sent in my portfolio.*

- *Pictures were taken for the portfolio; just to be sending them to Fairfield was exciting for me.*

- *I credit my friends who gave me the courage to embark on this "Fairfield Dream."*

- *The design for the skirt came to mind, long before the jacket. It came together in sections, first the skirt, then the jacket bodice, last of all the jacket sleeves.*

- *Many times when I've worked and dreamed about a garment for so long that I am not sure "if it's really good". Not with this one, "Starlight Rhapsody" was more than I hoped it would be.*

- *I ran the machine needle through my finger once in this project.*

- *I was new to detailed machine quilting before I started this garment, but after stitching 10 spools of Sulky Sliver, I feel I had a grasp on this technique.*

- *I loved using the Prismatic foil & getting to know Meryl Ann Butler. I struggled with a gummed up machine needle, but after I read the directions (one of the big faults in my life) and learned about needle lubricant (Sewer's Aid on page 13)- I had a great time making it do fun things for me.*

- *I'm a Fairfield Designer because of encouraging friends. When I teach or lecture; that will be the important point I stress, encouraging others, it may open doors of opportunity for someone by giving them the courage to walk thru those doors.*

- *Because of this experience my design imagination*

This elegant evening suit is a pieced collection of star blocks, several were taken from two books by Catherine Anthony and Libby Lehman, "Quiltmaker's Book of 6" Block Patterns (1986) and Sampler Supreme (1983). Drawing of these 6" blocks are illustrated below. Large sheets of graph paper were taped together; then the jacket and skirt designs were drawn.

Because adequate front bodice space was needed to show off the pieced stars, a side front opening was designed. Because the 6" star blocks on the jacket were so detailed, quick piece methods were used. The jacket had 549 separate pieces, all cut from templates.

The skirt is a six gore skirt, each with an identical star block panel. The panels lapped over into each other to give a continuous design. The panels each contained 166 pieces, all cut from templates. That made 996 pieces for the skirt.

Ten gold lamé and metallic fabrics were used in the star blocks, with a black and gold star design fabric as the background.

The ensemble is embellished with black Sulky Sliver thread, narrow gold braid and wire edged ribbon. The ribbon was accented with small gold beads. The buttons were faces of the sun in gold.

Prismatic foil created the illusion of running lights on the jacket and skirt. It sparkled as crystals under the runway lights. 450 amber faux jewels were glued (Aileen's Jewel It) on the jacket and skirt. To add detailing, 60 yards of narrow gold trim outlined all major designs.

Not long after the photos were taken and the garment was shipped to Fairfield, I presented a lecture to a guild in western Nebraska. Afterwards a woman asked me "when I knew it was finished". That was hard to answer but I told her, "it was finished when it felt right". "Starlight Rhapsody" felt right. What a wonderful life experience the whole process was to me.

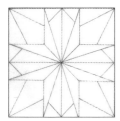 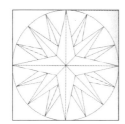 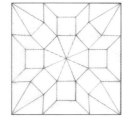 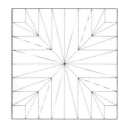 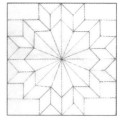

"Joseph Jubilation, Splendeur of Galaxias" 1995 Fairfield Fashion Show

This ensemble is a celebration of the scripture in Genesis that speaks of Joseph's coat of many colors. The word Splendeur is French for the English word splendor. I used the French because of it's beautiful sound when spoken; it means a "grand display". Galaxias is Latin for galaxy. If you squint your eyes, the color bars appear to float in space. This is because of the strong background fabric.

The cape was created using rainbow Pointillist Palette fabrics from Debbie Lunn and Antique Metallic from Spiegel, a black and gold star for the background fabric. Approximately 37 1/2 yards. of 100% cotton fabric was used and 2064 right triangle squares were made to create the color design called Radiating Triangles.

Pattern Trace was used to draw the design for the cape. Small squares representing each of the 2064 right triangle squares to be used were drawn. The biggest challenge was designing so that there was a perfect match at the side seams. It took great effort, but in the end everything matched to perfection.

Because of the massive size of the cape front and back, two design walls were needed. I was still in my old studio where I had no design wall space when Joseph's was made. A hall wall near my studio served as one design wall. I had to step back into a bedroom to see the wall, it was tight, but it worked. For the second design wall, a carpenter built me a portable wall I could hang from hooks in the ceiling of my small studio. It was cumbersome, but it worked for this project. I had to view the designs at a distance to see what was "really happening."

In the beginning the cape was to be calf length. I soon realized I would not be happy with that length, so the design was modified to the floor. More right triangle squares were assembled and added to the design.

Before the machine quilting began, the side seams were stitched. I worked to match each little color intersection; it was a tedious job, but because of accurate drafting of the design, it went together perfectly. A twin needle and matching metallic thread was used to stitch each color wave. Because the color waves started and stopped in the middle of the cape, this was a tremendous job. The same as quilting on a odd shaped queen-king size quilt.

Next it was embellished with prismatic foil, faux jewels and 126 yards of sequin trim to match the colors waves.

The cape is lined with five colors of Dupioni silk, that when revealed, resembles unfurled butterfly wings. See pictures of this lining on page 120.

The dress is made of black Dupioni. When the dress was assembled, the back seam was left open. It was embellished with jewel toned variegated Sulky Sliver thread and a twin needle. The stitching is done in a flowing manner that that starts on a lower section, then curves up the front and ends up at upper back on the left back section. The stitching accentuates the slender curved lines of the dress. A three toned Dupioni flounce accents the back of the dress. The flounce was designed not for just the additional color, but also to give ease through the hips for the different models that would wear it that year. A rainbow of sequin trim embellishes the neck band.

Joseph's Jubilation is an original work and took 200 hours to complete.

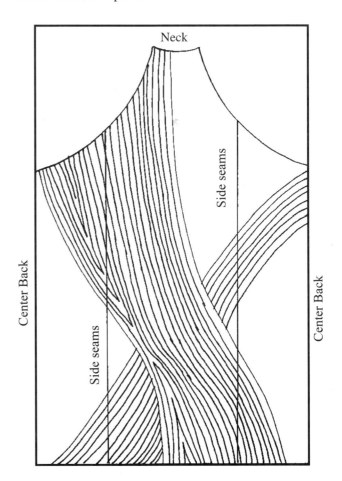

"Arabesque" 1997 20th Anniversary Fairfield Fashion Show

Arabesque ....
A complex and ornate design of intertwined floral, foliate and geometrical figures.

At the end of December 1996, I received a letter from the producers of the Fairfield Fashion Show requesting I be a part of their 20th Anniversary Show, in November of 1998. Because Fairfield had plans for a book to celebrate this special show, our garments were to be shipped by September 1, 1997...15 months before the show premiered. "Arabesque" would be away for two years. I felt very honored to be a part of this select group of men and women.

So you have a feel for how life was at the Raymond household in 1997, in late February, our daughter Mary Karol became engaged. The wedding was scheduled for late July as both MK and Craig were teachers. I had already accepted the invitation to the Fairfield show and now we are going to have a wedding. It all came off as scheduled, but it was a hard summer. Not much time for chasing butterflies in my garden.

Commercial patterns were used for the basic shapes in the garments, but everything else is original in design.

The evening dress was designed first, and is made from hot pink crepe backed satin, with the crepe side on top. The color was perfect but the satin too shiny. The skirt is embellished with random twin needle stitching using Sulky's hot pink Sliver thread. The bodice is embellished with hand-dyed silk ribbon flowers. Flowers were also made from silks and satins using the rolled hem function on my serger to finish the edges. Very thin wire was sewn in with the rolled hem so I could make the fabric take shape just like the purchased wire edged ribbon. The flowers are embellished with seed beads for the flower centers. The bodice is further embellished with silk ribbons and purchased satin leaves.

The Evening Cloak was great fun to dream up and design. It includes two capes, one long and trailing, the other one is fingertip length and designed to resembled sleeves.

The January before this garment was made, I saw "Phantom of the Opera". There is a scene where Christine comes strolling onto the stage in a hooded cape, that was dragging the floor and had a slight train. I knew this was what I wanted to make for this show.

Arabesque is made from over 100 different cotton fabrics. See page 76. Included are ten kaleidoscope stars in the cape design. Each section of the six point star sections was broken down many times, to include as much color and fabric design as possible. Several sections in each star point are "fussy cut", a favorite technique included in my work.

The star on the back of the fingertip length cape took over six hours to design, cut out and sew. It was worth the effort because the final results are so wonderful. The caplet and lower cape are machine quilted using a twin needle and Sulky Sliver thread. Both are embellished with designer threads and yarns. The caplet is embellished with black fringe and gold braid on the outside edge and small pieces of prismatic foil to catch the lights while on the runway.

Shoulder pads were used as the foundation of the epaulets. Tassels made of designer threads, ribbons and Sulky threads make up the fringe. The roses are made from hand-dyed silk wire edged ribbon, as well as ribbon I made from silks and satins. The epaulets are embellished with leaves made from ribbon.

Both the dress and cape were hung on a dress form, then the flowers and leaves were placed on the garments. It made placement of the flowers so much easier, because it showed me exactly where the flowers would be on a person's body. I did not want the roses to show up in "funny places" - it might have broken up the style show mood in Houston.

The cape is lined in hand-painted fabric. A quick little story about this fabric. A show sponsor offered to hand paint fabrics for the designers. I worked hard at sending her samples of colors, etc., but when the fabric arrived, it just did not fit my vision for this garment. Omigosh, it was June and I had a wedding come up, no time to travel to Lincoln or Omaha to find other fabric, so.....I covered my pool table with paint drop clothes, taped the painted fabric to the drop clothes, and repainted the lining fabric. I had no idea what I was doing, but it turned out just like I wanted it to in the first place. Over the fabric paint, I embellished with glitter paint, glitter, sponge painting and jewels.

Arabesque was fun to make because of the great collection of fabrics and the gorgeous kaleidoscope stars. With each garment, new ideas or techniques are tried, With Arabesque, the new techniques were the flowers and kaleidoscope stars. I was very happy with the results.

This ensemble consists of four pieces, an evening coat, two detachable ribbon fur collars, and an evening gown. With the exception of the TWE beads that embellish the bodice of the evening gown and some hand work, every single stitch was sewn on my Bernina. I love the way my Bernina reacts just the way I need it to at any given moment. It will get into tight little corners, sew round seams, whatever I demand of it and do so with accuracy and finesse, with this project it was put to the test.

The evening gown is a regal Vogue Pattern that was perfect for what I wanted to make. I have longed admired Caryl Bayer Faller's work and wanted the dress to reflect her type of design.

I traced the pattern pieces onto Pattern Trace, a Pellon product. The dress is a floor length slender sheath with 7 body sections. These were pinned together the at the seam lines.

Next I drew free hand the design on the dress, working to create a free flowing design with interlocking color areas that include black, purple, kiwi, fuchsia and jade. The sections are broken down into separate areas to include 4-5 shades of each color.

My challenge for this project was to sew only curved lines. This made for very tedious piecing of the garment. When I started this project, I had no idea what I was doing; but I patiently worked through the process and feel it was a great success.

After drawing the design area on the dress section, I again traced the whole pattern onto Pattern Trace. Next I cut each small section apart to piece the dress, this was another big learning curve for me. Grain of fabric on each small section was noted, then I free hand cut out each section, adding seam allowance as I went. I worked in small sections, to not become totally confused. Each seam was marked with hash marks in the middle of the curves and dots at the intersecting points, so all would sew back together accurately. The design for the dress sleeves were taken from a stained glass pattern book.

When I reviewed the many stitches available on the 180, I discovered a built in stipple stitch, what good fortune! It took over 20 hours to machine quilt the dress alone, but the built in stitch saved my hands and arms from getting tired, the machine did the work for me. The dress was quilted with metallic thread to match each color family.

Embellishing the bodice of the evening gown are TWE beads and crystals. They are accented with a medallion made with a decorative stitch from the 180 and Sulky Sliver in the companion color. The Sliver gave more "punch" to the crystals and beads, to help them be seen from the audience.

The coat is a McCalls pattern with high collar. It is made of Dupioni silk with stained glass design work in varied shades of fuchsia, kiwi, jade and purple. The batting is Fairfield Soft Touch. Machine quilting included free motion stipple; using a variety of Sulky threads; including black Sliver, rayon in complementary colors, jewel-toned variegated Sliver and various metallic threads. Some of the free motion stitching was sewn with a twin needle. A beautiful hand-dyed ribbon with metallic edging was stitched on the coat to create a jagged, zig-zag design.

Sulky's Ultra Water Soluble Solvy was used to create Confetti fabric to embellish the coat. See page 87 for this technique. Small scraps of Dupioni silk, Sulky metallic, rayon and Sliver threads, variegated pearl cotton from YLI plus various yarns and threads were used to create the Confetti fabric. It embellished the cuffs, below the collar and down the front a short distance. Medallions of the fabric were scattered on the back.

The focal points of the coat are the detachable collars. They are covered with 450 yards of flowing streamers of Offray satin ribbons in the colors of the ensemble; they resemble long strands of jewel toned satin fur. To keep the ribbons from fraying, I soaked each ribbon tip in Fray Check. The sleeves were sewn with layers of ribbons as well; along with the collars, there are flowing waves of color on each side of the coat.

The coat lining is taffeta. The design was stitched using a twin needle and decorative stitches on the Bernina 180. A different rayon thread thread was used in each needle, switching to different colors with each new decorative stitch sewing line. The designs within the squares are stenciled with fabric paint.

Finishing the coat is multi-colored piping (page) made of the many colors of Dupioni. A handmade frog (page 116) made of the same pipping fabric, embellishes the front opening along with one large black button.

"Diamonds are a Girl's Best Friend"
2002 Bernina Fashion Show - Viewer's Choice Award

Very seldom in life is anything "easy" and making Diamonds was no exception. I had no preconceived design ideas about this show because I didn't expect to receive an invitation. The theme "Masquerade"; brought to mind the harlequin design and a black and winter white silk Dupioni coat. My first dilemma was an interesting coat pattern, nothing I found spoke to me. Next, I rummaged through my collection of old patterns and I found an old robe pattern, I knew I could make it work. After hours of "manipulating" the pattern it was time to play with fabrics.

The harlequin design starts as small squares at the bottom of the coat; each row graduates in size until the center diamond is about 7" long, then it tapers back as it goes to the top of the coat. Many hours were spent, measuring and remeasuring, making sure all was going to match just as it should.

After piecing the coat, which was no small task, it was time to embellish the garment. Fairfield's thin cotton batting with a poly organza foundation fabric was used. I knew the coat would be heavy and the organza helped to eliminate bulk. The layers were basted together with Sulky's KK 2000; such a time saver.

Sulky's silver metallic thread was stipple machine quilted on the white diamonds. Over the stipple quilting, a small diamond motif of faux sequined fabric was fused with Wonder Under. Aileen's Jewel It was applied with a small paint brush to seal the outside edges of the diamond motifs.

The red yokes, sleeve accents and front panels were created with four shades of red Dupioni, the dress fabric and Sulky's Ultra Solvy. What a fun product, with great results. See page 87 for more information.

The "Confetti Fabric" was attached to the coat with the bobbin draw technique, using red pearl cotton in the bobbin. To add width, two rows of feather stitches were sewn on the outside edge, over lapping each other. Last from the top, free motion stitching of red Sulky Holoshimmer. See page 92 for this technique.

Matching the side seams and raglan sleeves to the body sections was a big concern for me. After much contemplation, measuring and remeasuring, I cut out the coat and everything matched up perfectly. It happened because I was patient with the process.

The facings of the coat are black Dupioni and were stipple quilted with red pearl cotton. The lining is black satin and it was machine quilted with a 6.0 double needle using red Holoshimmer thread from Sulky. Custom labels were made using the monogram feature on the Bernina 180.

"Stuffed" (page 107) hand-made bound button holes were created, as well as multi-colored piping (page 115) around the outside edge of the coat. Cable cord used by upholsterers was used for the piping. I recommend its use, it's heavier and makes a firm edge. To hide the machine stitching on the piping, I hand blind stitched each side of the piping to the coat front and then the facing. Since the garment was being judged, I didn't want the stitching to show.

Gorgeous rhinestone buttons complement the front opening that lap over to the left shoulder. Another point of interest is the original design collar.

The Designer Vogue pattern from Sassoon was perfect for the red metallic sheer fabric purchased in Dallas for the evening gown. The dress features a shaped bodice, bias cut skirt with back pleats, applied flounce and a shaped back hemline. The dress was underlined and lined. Because of the draping ability of the fabric, the view from the back is awesome.

The coat and dress are embellished with 850 Swarovski Crystal Rhinestones using rim sets, each applied by hand.

Crystal waterfall necklace, earrings and tiara are perfect elements to finish off the design.

The realization came to me after all the work, that it takes many steps to make an ensemble such as this and each is tedious and slow. The work can not be hurried. I worked several 15 hours days, and what I thought would take me two days, in reality took five. To do "it right" took patience and TIME. In the end it was worth the lost sleep. After 230 hours of work - "Diamonds are a Girls' Best Friend" was complete and I just wanted a long summer's nap.

Embellishments . . . .

> *Jenny's dictionary says:*
> *Any accent used to decorate wearables: hand or machine quilting, appliqué,*
> *trims, manipulations of fabric & fabric design, thread work, glitz, paint,*
> *jewels, buttons, beads, charms, prismatic foil, linens, yarn & fabric flowers:*
> ***anything*** *to which one's Creative Being says* ***YES!*** Let the fun begin!

Always make a sample . . . .

Over time I have discovered the importance of making samples for all wearable and sewing projects. A sample could be as follows: top fabric, batting & foundation fabric. I sandwich these fabrics as if for an actual project, then make samples of stitching, buttonholes, whatever needs to be tested.. It's important to "audition" with all the layers, because if it is not the same as the actual project, you will not get the same results as you would on your project.

As an example, when I made "From Nebraska with Love", I wanted to use decorative stitches from the Bernina 180 to embellish the black satin lining for the coat. My idea was to use a criss-cross design similar to the following illustration. For picture see page 76.

Using a twin needle with Decorator Stitches on Machine

I cut a swatch of the black satin lining fabric and kept it by my machine. I wanted to try something new. Using a twin needle and the many decorator stitches on my machine. I auditioned many stitch and rayon thread combinations. When I had a combination I liked, then I stitched on the lining sections. After completely stitching the grid, which was a big process, I hung the lining on my design wall.

The next step was to add small stenciled motifs as illustrated. I made many samples of several different stencil patterns and paint combinations; then I auditioned the small samples in the squares before I actually applied the paint to the lining. I placed the different samples on the grid, and walked away to see which one I liked the best. After I made my careful decision, then I stenciled the lining. Once the paint was on the lining, it was there for good.

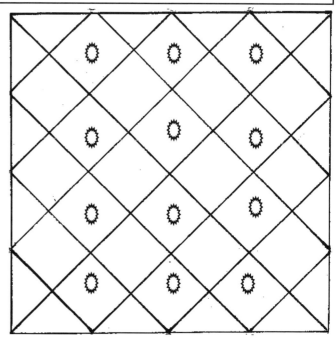

I suggest you audition anything that might have to be ripped out: machine quilting and embellishments, to check for correct machine tension and if you like what you see. Check how your fabric reacts to Fray Check, Sewer's Aid or any product or technique you are not sure about.

It is especially important to audition buttonholes, using the exact combination of top, facing fabric and interfacing to work your sample. This will tell you if you are going to have any small problems. You will know ahead of time, instead of when you are working on center front of your garment.

You will never regret taking the time to make samples. I've learned to have patience in my work and it is one of the reasons my work has improved.

Fabric Manipulations.............................

Fabric manipulations include all sorts of ways of using fabric in a manner, it was never intended. It's a matter of bending the "will" of the fabric to our own. An example would be teenage daughter who we want to behave one way and she definitely wants to behave another. In the case of fabric, we win.

Wrinkling, Crinkling, Pushing & Shoving

For the 2001 AQS Fashion Show, I designed "Sand hills Melody" a jacket, blouse and slacks. Page 46.

The jacket was made from 27 different colors of Dupioni silk. It is a collage of manipulated fabric. Primarily I used the technique where fabric is soaked in water, then crimped into tight folds, twisted, tied and dried. Of course I never do "anything easy" and each section was pieced in a different design. For instance the collar was pieced in a crazy quilt design. I pieced small blocks then sewed them together in a section large enough for the upper collar, then I soaked, folded, twisted, tied and dried.

Above are pictures of the different sections I pieced, then manipulated. Because of the delicate nature of the silk, I sergered all seams on the back of the piecing, I knew that if I did not, my seams would not hold up under the stress of manipulation.

Pleat the wet fabric section as you would a paper fan. Close the fan, so that the folds are tight. Next hold

both ends and twist, then tie the twist together as best you can. Use scraps of fabric or string to hold the twisted and tied section together.

Bubble Fabric

On a teaching trip to Rapid City, SD I discovered a great technique. A vest was on display and the fabric had been manipulated into little bubbles. I had no idea how to accomplish this, but knew I wanted to find out. I asked around and was given the name of a book. It is now out of print and that's too bad as it was full of great fabric manipulation ideas. To create "Bubbled Fabric" you first purchase a cookie cooling rack with a grid, such as is illustrated to the right.

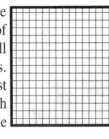

Lay the fabric face down on the rack. Do this by a sink because the fabric must be kept soaking wet. I poured water on as I worked. Use a wooden pencil with an eraser, and start in the middle of the fabric, then poke the fabric thru the squares. This takes patience, but it's worth the effort. After you have the fabric poked through as much as you can, it's time to dry the fabric. My cooling rack was too big for my dehydrator, let me tell you how I discovered the perfect place to dry this fabric.

We have a small half bath off our kitchen. This little room has electric heat and in the winter it's like a sauna. My husband is cold natured and turns the heat up to 10. When I walk in, it takes my breath away; so I turn it back down. Ah ha! I realized I found the perfect place to dry my rack of fabric, I turned up the heat, placed the rack on the sink counter, walked away and at the end of the day it was dry.

Do not take the fabric out of the rack! I know you are excited to see the results but the next step is very important. Iron fusible interfacing on the back of the bubbled section, while it is still on the rack. Now you can take the fabric out of the rack. To help stabilize this section, I stitched between every three or four rows with .004 nylon thread. Use your zipper foot for this step and it will not smash the bubbles.

My "bubbled fabric" was used on the sleeves of my jacket. Now I want to make a vest using this technique. Just think of the questions people will have for me. How did you do that? You must try this, it's really fun.

Drying the fabric sections

Since the mid 80s I've had a large food dehydrator. When I first purchased it, I dried fruit from our orchard and vegetables. Now I seldom use it now for what it was intended. It's great for drying small fabric project, such as fabric manipulations, broom stick skirts, etc.

The machine I have is no longer on the market, but if you are interested in purchasing one for this type of project, you will need a larger dehydrator than is common on the market. I searched the web and found the L'Equip 528 Food Dehydrator. It's available from several difference sources, enter L'Equip into a search engine and you will find many vendors from which to purchase. I use mine for a lot of different projects: fabric manipulations, confetti fabric (page 87), plus green peppers and apples in the fall.

L'Equip 528 Food Dehydrator

Raggedy Edge Appliqué

This is a fun idea using various medallions of fabric. The illustration shows fairly large medallions of fabric but in reality you might want to use smaller, as you "play" you will be able to make that decision.

This type of project could be made on a sweatshirt base as well as a basic pattern. A really great print would be wonderful to completely cover the sweatshirt or pattern, then pick up all the different colors in the raggedy appliqué. Stitch patches 1/4" from the edge of fabric.

Embellished raggedy appliqué: If your machine has embroidery abilities, you could embroidery in the middle of the medallions. Even simple stipple stitching would be great in a variegated thread that picked up the colors in your fabrics would be interesting. Use water soluble stabilizer with this project.

Love

Raw Edge Appliqué

"The Garden of Eden"
Color Picture Page 46

When spring arrives, I eagerly check my gardens for the first signs of early crocus. Next comes daffodils, tulips and the many spring bulbs that are planted in my garden. This is one of my most favorite times of year. It was during just such a spring that "The Garden of Eden" was born.

Over the years there have been many gorgeous garments in the Fairfield and Bernina Fashion Show that featured this type of appliqué. I wanted to give this a try and what better theme than one of the passions in my life, flowers.

I had a great lime green fabric on hand and decided that it would be the foundation for this garment. I pre washed all the fabrics for this project, so they wouldn't shrink on me later.

I used Butterick 5555 for the long duster coat and a simple sheath pattern for the dress. The coat pattern was designed with set in sleeves and notched jacket collar. I changed the pattern to have high slits on the side seams. I sewed the shoulder seams together before I started the flower design.

I had a big selection of floral fabrics, some from when I had my fabric store in the 80's. I pressed fusible web on the back of the fabric, then cut out the flowers and leaves. I hung the coat on my dress form and placed the flowers as it hung, using long quilting pins to secure. It took hours to cut out all the flowers and audition them, but in the end it was worth all the time and effort. I placed flowers on the upper collar, under collar, lapel, body sections and down the sleeves. Bugs and butterflies were tucked among the flowers and leaves.

After the flowers were finally in the perfect arrangement, I fused them in place. This is a spring coat so to avoid using a foundation fabric or batting, I placed a water soluble material under the whole coat. To help eliminate the problem of having to deal with so much fabric under the machine, I rolled and folded the sections not being sewn.

Using my open toe free motion foot, I stitched around each flower motif with rayon thread. I practiced on a sample first to get the hang of doing this type of stitch. After practice, the free motion stitch just breezed around each design. When the outline stitch was complete, I stitched free motion thread painting over the flowers and leaves. This took many hours of stitching but again, it was worth it with the end result. Because of the soluble stabilizer used under the whole project, all of the stitching was even and smooth with no puckering.

The next step was to soak away the soluble material in the bathtub. After the soluble product was completely dissolved, I hung the coat pieces to dry.

Them it was time to press and complete the construction of the coat. I used fuchsia lining for the coat and made a dress out of the lime green.

After the coat was finished and pressed, I decided it needed a few beads. I fell back to my neat little "quick trick" with Aileen's Jewell It. I created clusters of beads in the centers of some of the flower using the glue and an assortment of beads. See page 96 on how to make the flower centers.

This concept could be made with many different theme fabrics. I can see a great Christmas jacket or any holiday; how about an ocean full of fish, a sky full of birds or a forest of animals. Start dreaming about this project, I know you can come up with a great idea.

A Vest for All Season is also made with this technique. See picture on page 53.

Shadow Appliqué

Shadow *Appliqué* is a beautiful manipulation to use on a vest, bodice of dress or jacket. Our example will be a shadow appliqué collar and you will need the following. A collar pattern, light colored base fabric, the appliqué design, voile or very sheer fabric and under collar fabric. There are many appliqué patterns available for your use.

 # 1 - Cut the collar pattern from the voile, base fabric, and under collar fabric. Lay your base fabric on a flat surface.

 # 2 - Now arrange your appliqué design. Use bright colors for your appliqué, as the voile will tone them down. Use Wonder Under or like product to secure the appliqué design.

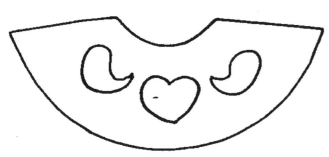

 # 3 - Lay the voile on top of your base-appliqué design layer. Baste around the outside edge of collar, making sure all is straight and even. Next stitch around the outside of each appliqué design. I suggest you drop the feed dogs use your open toe free motion foot and free motion stitch around each motif. For this stitching I suggest you use any of the gorgeous Sulky rayon threads.

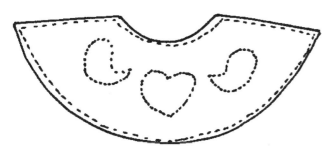

 # 4 - Assemble the back portion of your collar as you did the front: base and voile. Sew the front and backs of top layers of collar together at the shoulder seams. Do the same for the under collar. Lay both collar sections right sides together and sew outside edges as indicated on your pattern. You are ready to apply finished collar to your garment.

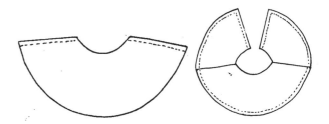

Silk Flower Shadow Appliqué

I recently bought a shirt with a new technique I had not seen before. Petals from silk/polyester flowers were used for appliqué, over the flower petals was a layer of chiffon. The shirt is black with black chiffon sewn over the flowers. See picture of appliqué on page 46.

It appears the centers of the flower were stitched in place with tailor tacks; through many washings the flowers have not come loose. I have not tried this but know it will work. Try this as a sample.

- Take one silk flower and carefully take apart. I would put the flower in water to make sure it washes ok.
- Cut a 6" square of washable fabric. Lay flower sections from the disassembled silk flower on the fabric. For your first sample use only one layer of petals.
- Use the tacking stitch on your machine to secure the centers of the fabric.
- This next step is simply a guess but I would use a little Aileen's Jewel It along the bottom edge of the flower petals. Press into the bottom fabric.
- Cover with a 6" square of chiffon the same color as bottom fabric. Stitch around the outside edge. What do you think? I can hardly wait to try this out, I know it's going to work.

Confetti Fabric - *Creating Your Own Fabric with Water Soluble Stabilizer.*

What a fun way to use up even the smallest scraps of fabric from a wearable project. I first used this process on my 2001 Bernina ensemble "From Nebraska with Love". The dress and coat were made of many different silk Dupioni fabric, I saved every little scrap in a bag.

Confetti Fabric Sample

Cut 1 - 12"x24" section water soluble stabilizer into two 12" x 12" sections. Lay one section on your working table; spray with adhesive.

Cut a piece of print fabric 12"x12", lay on top of bottom section of stabilizer.

Using your rotary cutter and mat, cut your selection of fabrics into small pieces. Do not make them too small, I would say no smaller than 1".

Arrange fabric pieces on top of the print fabric If you desire lay designer threads and yarns, and strands of metallic and rayon threads on top of the fabrics.

Add a few more pieces of fabric and include some circles. Adding a few circles on top of the blunt cut sections, helps to visually smooth out the sharp edges. When you think it's just as you want it, lightly spray adhesive over the fabrics and trims. Press second sheet of stabilizer onto fabrics. Press all layers together.

Use nylon (.004) thread to sew a grid over your "Confetti Fabric" section as illustrated to the right. Stitch 2-3" apart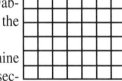

Now it is time to highly machine quilt and embellish this section. I start by doing random twin needle machine quilting, then fill my bobbin with pearl cotton or rayon and stitch a little bobbin draw in a stipple stitch. Next I heavily embellish with designer threads and yarns.

If you've used spray adhesive, let your Confetti Fabric set for several days so that it can dissipate, otherwise there could be a residue on your fabric.

Soak your Confetti Fabric section according to the package instructions for the soluble stabilizer you used. Rinse well and let dry. If I am in a hurry, this is another time where I use my food dehydrator. Page 84.

Press well. Cut a section of fusible web to fit your Confetti Fabric, then press in place. On the paper back of the fusible web, draw sections such as illustrated to below. Cut out sections. Have fun arranging these medallions on your newest creation.

88

Projects using Confetti Fabric

"From Nebraska with Love"
Page 76

A technique I was anxious to try and decided to include on this ensemble was making my own fabric using water soluble stabilizer. I learned a lot the first time around and have totally changed my method. With all the piecing that was done with "from Nebraska with Love" I had a shopping bag full of scraps. The biggest mistake I made was to cut the fabrics up into tiny little pieces, they were hard to control and keep in one place. I cut the pieces bigger now, at least 1" square.

I used the Confetti Fabric under the stand up collar on the coat, at the cuff on the coat sleeve and several medallions on the coat. The following pictures, illustrate how I decided on the right shape and size for use under the collar. I cut pieces of Pellon pattern trace into interesting shapes. Pattern trace is a great product that I use often. I not only trace patterns that I modify but use it for projects such as the embellishment pattern on this coat.

I hung the coat on my dress form, then pinned on the shapes. I was able to reshape until they were "perfect". Then I used them as the pattern to cut out the Confetti Fabric. Because I knew they were the perfect fit around the neck, I did not waste any of my hard earned confetti fabric.

"Diamonds are a Girl's Best Friend"
Page 76

Making Confetti Fabric for "Diamonds" was an enormous project because I needed so much of it.

Many hours were spent drafting the yoke areas on the coat for the Confetti fabric. To work out the details, I used Pattern Trace in the same manner I used it on from NE with Love. I cut the pattern for these areas

out of pattern trace, then laid the patterns on the garment pattern to be certain of a good fit.

All of the red trim on the coat is Confetti fabric. I purchased four different shades of red Dupioni silk for this project and included the red evening fabric with a metallic thread woven in to give it shimmer. I used one of the red silks as the bottom layer of fabric, then cut larger pieces of all the reds to create just the perfect look.

The next step was to twin needle machine quilt in a random manner. I purchased 12 skeins of red pearl cotton and used the bobbin draw technique to stipple stitch over the entire area.

While on a teaching trip to New York, I found gorgeous heavy red yarns from a vendor at the quilt show where I was working. After the machine quilting and bobbin drawn, I couched these yarns over the whole area.

I cannot tell you what a difficult job this was. When I ordered the stabilizer for this project from Sulky, I ordered the Super Heavy and that was a mistake. It made the confetti fabric sections heavy and hard to get under my machine. I can see where this product would be great for small projects, but when you are creating large sections, it is just too heavy. It was a job getting the Solvy dissolved and completely rinsed. I should have ordered the Super Solvy which is a lighter weight.

Once it was dry, then the real fun began. It was worth all the effort because of how gorgeous the final results turned out to be. It was perfect.

I am happy with the looks of the confetti fabric on the coat and the design I used to showcase it. You can tell from the sketch of the coat and the dark areas where I used the confetti fabric and how much I had to make.

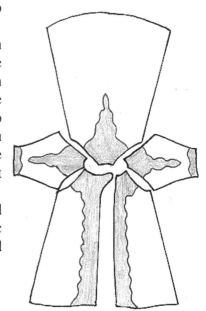

Plaid & Stripe Magic

Two of my favorite designs of fabric are plaids and stripes. I love the beautiful play of color. During the years I owned my fabric store, I made an interesting discovery about manipulating these kinds of fabric.

It works well with stripes or plaids. For the novice I suggest you start with an even plaid or stripe. The idea is to create a chevron design for use on back yokes, cuffs, and pockets. This same concept can be used in piecing quilts. Perhaps you will discover other uses.

 # 1 - The first step is to lay the fabric right side up on a flat working area.

 # 2 - Next lay the fabric back on itself. Do this from right to left. You will fold back from 1/3 to 1/2 yd. Remember to fold the fabric **back on itself**. As you repeat this process, you will be able to gauge how much to fold.

 # 3 -Next draw a stitching line on the back side of the fabric as illustrated. Now take sewing pins, pin through the fabric and match up your stripe or plaid to the exact match on the under fabric. Pin along stitching line at all important intersecting points. When you have a perfect match, stitch along marked line over pins if your machine will allow.

 # 4 - Next fold back edge of fabric to see if your match is exact. I'm going to be cranky here, if it doesn't match perfectly, take it out and do over.

 # 5 - When you are happy with your Chevron design, lay the center line of your pattern piece along the stitching line on your fabric. Make sure all is correct, then cut.

It's a good idea at this point to stabilize the back of your Chevron piece with fusible interfacing as it is cut on the bias. My favorite fusible interfacing is Pellon 800F.

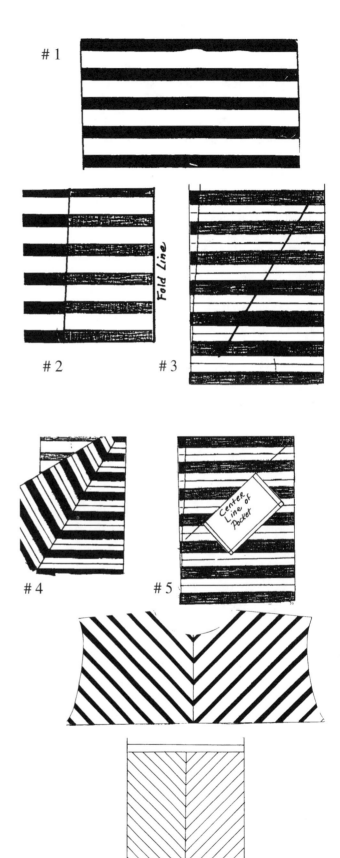

Machine Thread..

Metallic and Rayon Thread

In 1994 when I was working on "Starlight Rhapsody" my first Fairfield Fashion Show Ensemble, I discovered volumes about these threads. From my experience, they are not all created equally. I have used a number of brands and find that the Sulky brand works every time, the way it should. Several hints to successful use of metallic thread are:

1. Use a sharp # 12 or #14 Needle. I use universal needles with success, but it is important to buy good ones. I suggest Schmetz. If threads continue to break, you may have a needle that is defective. I read that the eye of the needle can have a burr, causing the thread to break. If all else fails and you keep breaking thread, change the needle.
2. Check that the tension and timing of your machine is correct. Your machine dealer might be the one to do this for you, if you are not familiar with your machine's workings.
3. I use a liquid silicon product called Sewers Aid. Place a drop of this at the top of your needle, it will assist in machine stitching with metallic and rayon threads. I use Sewer's Aid on the spool of thread as well. Squeeze three spaced rows of liquid across the spool.
4. Keep the bobbin and bobbin hook area very clean. When this area gets dirty your threads may start to break. Keep clean and oiled according to your machine directions. Clean with compressed air every time you change your bobbin.
5. I find that metallic threads feed better when positioned in a vertical manner. You will need to judge this by your machines performance. See photo & more information to the right.
6. Problems can arise with the use of spray adhesives and products with special backings. It is possible for a build up to occur on the machine needle, making for added tension on the thread. Sewer's Aid may be the answer for this problem.
7. Last of all, occasionally I believe there's a bad spool of thread. If it continues to break and you have tried changing your needle, it's probably a defective spool of thread. I know this hurts, but throw it away.

Sewing Thread

Machine thread is the one product, we cannot sew without. Often it causes distress because of problems that can arise. One fact I learned during my "Sewing Basket" years was that you get what you pay for when it comes to thread. I never sold "3 spools for a $1.00" thread. Cheap thread stretches as it travels through your machine, then throws off your tension, it also deteriorates over time. Quality threads holds up better and is well worth the additional cost.

Nylon Thread

For so long the stitch quality of nylon thread left much to be desired; it was too heavy, no better than fishing line. Today .004 nylon thread is available; it is fine as a hair and works beautifully. It's available in clear and smoke colors. I've been successful in using nylon thread in my bobbin, you should try it sometime.

Hand Sewing Thread

A number of years ago I discovered quilting thread for hand sewing. I use it for sewing buttons, snaps, hems, just about everything. I keep every color available to use on all my projects. It is strong and holds much better than regular sewing thread.

Vertical Thread Holder

One day, I made a great discovery. I needed another vertical thread holder and my local Ben Franklin did not carry them. The perfect solution was sitting right next to my Bernina. My serger was the answer. I moved it close to my machine as pictured; then I can use two or more threads with ease whenever I use a double needle or even a triple needle.

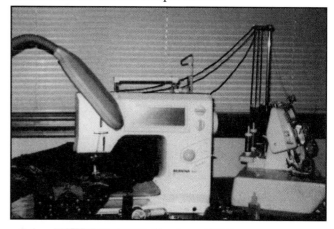

Twin Needle Free Form Quilting.........................

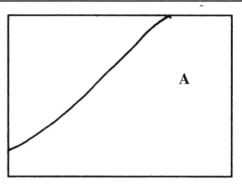

Make a sample before you stitch on a project, try the following first.

A. Make a 12 x 12 sandwich of fabric, batting and fabric. Next draw a line similar to the following with a disappearing pen or chalk pencil. Insert a twin needle into your machine, use two different colors of thread.

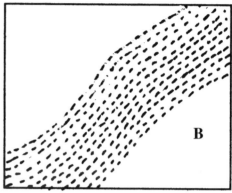

B. Starting at the left edge, use this line as your guide and stitch across your sample. When finished go back to the starting point and use your presser foot as your guide to sew a second line to the right of the first row. Keep the edge of your presser foot butted up against the right stitching line of first row. Sew slow until you get the feel. Sew 6 different double sewing rows.

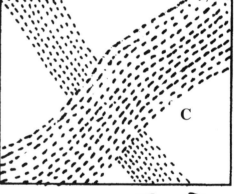

C. Next, mark another line coming in from a different direction. Stitch the same way as before but stop when you get to the previous stitching. Try to stitch right into the on coming row, back stitch two and then cut close the long threads. Jump over the first rows of stitching, back tack and continue stitching as illustrated.

D. Another way to stitch is to let the second stitching lines travel across the first stitching as illustrated on the dress.

When you finish stitching, secure threads in one of two ways:

1. Pull through loose threads through to the back and tie, secure with Fray Check.

2. If fabric will allow (test ahead of time, as this is done on the top) cut back tacked threads close to end of stitching and secure with Fray Check. See page 13 for info on this.

You may choose to use a double needle with random machine quilting, stippling, yes you can stipple with a double needle or the decorator stitches on your machine. For more ideas see pages 78-80 and 82. Pictures: page 75, last picture page 76, center picture and Blue Velvet on page 105.

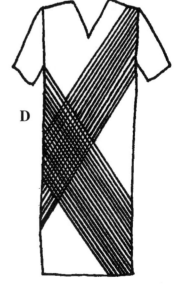

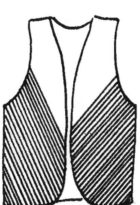

Bobbin Drawing

This is a great technique to utilize pearl cotton and rayon. There are so many of these products on the market, unbelievable color selection as well as variegated combinations.

Bobbin drawing is a very simple process whereby, the pearl thread is wound onto a bobbin. This requires loosing the tension on your bobbin casing. The first time I did this, I was scared I would mess up my machine, not a problem at all, it worked like a charm and the results was so beautiful. This is an example of something I hadn't tried, because I didn't think I could do it. I've learned that if I don't try, I won't know if a process is going to work. Because I use this technique so often I purchased a separate bobbin case just for bobbin draw.

I've auditioned several different thread types and they all worked great. They include metallic crochet thread, thin metallic designer threads, any other thread too big to go through the eye of your machine needle can probably be used. You will have to "carefully" experiment.

Because the thread is in the bottom, you're stitching with the right side down, underside up. Below is an example of the stipple stitch. For complete instructions and information, I highly recommend the book "Threadplay" by Libby Lehman.

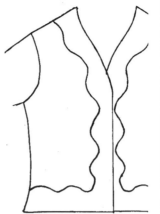 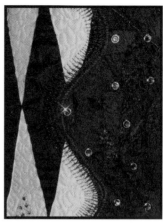

across the bottom. It continued on over the shoulder, down on the sleeves and ended on the jacket back in a scalloped medallion.

Diamonds are a Girl's Best Friend" (above right) has this same fabric embellishment. I wanted to accent the outside edge with decorative stitches from my machine but use pearl cotton in the bobbin. My dilemma was how to see the scallop on the underside of the garment. The following was my solution to this problem.

1. Fusible web was ironed to the underside of my scallop border. Next I fused the scallop border to the jacket section.
2. Then I edge stitched around the scallop design in thread that matched the scallop design and that would show up well on the reverse side of the garment.

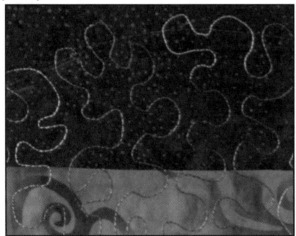

Decorative Stitches & Pearl Cotton or Rayon

It amazes me how so often the solution to a problem comes to me, when I take the time to visualize and think through the problem. Several years ago, I made a gorgeous silk jacket for a long time client in Maryland. It was made from a collection of natural toned silks. The picture at the top on the left is this jacket. An interesting design element for this jacket was a scalloped panel, almost a border around the jacket; down both fronts and

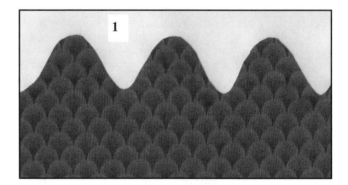

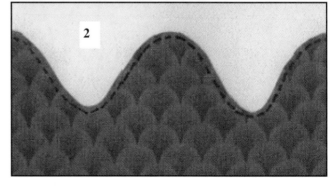

3. After the edge stitching was complete, I turned the garment to the inside, and the stitching line was visible on the underside.

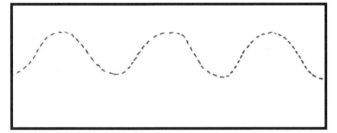

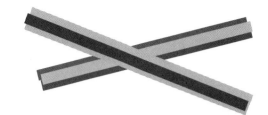

Because the pearl cotton was in the bobbin, my stitching would be done from the under side of the garment. I followed the stitching line so that my decorative stitches covered the outside scallops. To get an extra wide, heavy cover on the front of the garment, sew the decorative stitching rows several times. Stitch across once, then go back and stitch again, on the outside next to the first row. Below is an illustration of this.

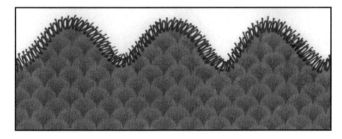

Double Needle Zigzag

This embellishment I dreamed up for "Sunrise, Sunset" on page 46. A double needle (2.00 - 2.50) along with two different colors of rayon thread were used.

Set your machine for a satin stitch. Experiment with your machine on stitch width & do so very carefully. Set stitch width for the widest zigzag possible, then turn the machine's wheel by hand to test, so that you don't break a needle.

I sewed this embellishment in long single rows with cross-bars. Experiment with length of design. Back tack and secure the threads at the beginning and end of the stitching with a half drop of Fray Check.

Next I placed a single needle in the machine with a third color of Sulky Rayon and sewed a very narrow satin stitch down the center of the first two rows of stitching. For "Sunrise, Sunset" on page 46, I used many different colors and the results were really great.

Designer Threads

When describing most of my garments, you have probably noticed how often I mention designer threads and yarns in this book. That's because I love what they do for my designs.

Designer, heavy threads and light weight yarns are all used to embellish garments. Today there are great assortments available.

This year, I became acquainted with "Adornaments" and all I can say is WOW. I've been asked by the ladies who own this company to use their products in several new original ideas, these will be displayed at Spring market 2004.

I've used the Designer Threads brand for many years and will continue to do so as each company has their own combinations, and each is necessary to cover the color range.

My wearables aren't complete without a "good dose" of designer threads and yarns. Use a zigzag stitch to sew them on, this is called couching. I prefer to use either .004 nylon or metallic thread to stitch the threads in place. I use the metallic if a plain thread needs a little sparkle.

They are sewn in a random manner as illustrated in the picture above from Sunrise, Sunset page 46.

Cord Quilting

This technique I discovered on a trip to Dallas several years ago. I call this embellishment cord quilting. The jacket on display in Dallas was a beautiful wool flannel. This technique can be done with a simple design or an intricate one. If you are interested in intricate designs, I suggest you look for continuous machine quilting designs.

For this project you will need: fabric, quilting design, marking pencil, basting thread, two spools of same color thread for machine quilting and #70 or #80 cable cord. If you have a small piece of wool, do a sample on it. Because of it's nature, it's works well for this process.

For an example, I will take you through this process on the back of a jacket.

#1 - Use a chalk pencil to mark the design on the inside of your back section.

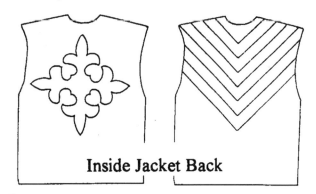

Inside Jacket Back

#2 - Find a good starting point on your design. Baste down #70 or #80 cable cord around the whole design. This is done on the inside of jacket following marked chalk pencil design. You need to baste with a contrasting color of thread right down the middle of the cable cord. They will be your stitching guide on the right side of fabric. They will be taken out when the process is finished.

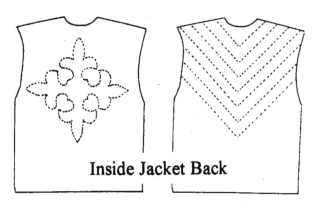

Inside Jacket Back

 # 3 - Turn your jacket over to the right side. Next insert a 3.0 double needle into your machine. You can use contrasting, variegated or matching thread to stitch the design. Using your double needle stitch either side of the cable cord from the top side. Experiment with thread tension. Adjust for best stitch quality. This is one time when you want a ridge to form.

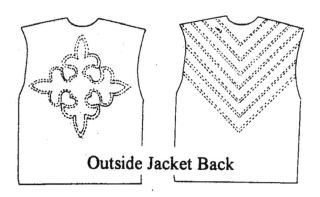

Outside Jacket Back

Thoughts on Batting Samples

(From the Internet - Stephanie Corina Goddard– Wed. May 2001 Member PACC. Used with permission.)

"I just did some experimenting with batting samples in preparation for a class and would like to pass along some of my observations:

Hobbs Wool Batting - I got this idea from a workshop given by Mary Ray. Mary showed us quilted garments that were flat enough to handle facings, collars and bound buttonholes. The trick is to make your quilt "sandwich" and press it firmly with an iron - before, during, and after machine quilting. It tried it over cotton and over rayon and it works beautifully.

Split batt - I'm anxious to try Larkin's suggestion of splitting a cotton batt, because I tried this with Mountain Mist Quilt Lite (a poly batt) and got strange results. The batt did not split evenly. Even though we're talking whisper thin layers, the difference was still noticeable in my samples. Moral of the story: you can split a poly batting, but make two piles and use all one side in a garment.

Flannel - I placed the flannel on the bias inside the sandwich and got a nice drape with both cotton and rayon. Hint: my "junk" flannel was striped, which made the bias placement oh so easy!

Ribbon as Embellishment

Ribbons can be a fun trim for garments, quilts, small gifts, accessories and home decorating. The following is information on a few varieties you might want to use:

Ombre: These ribbons shade from one edge to the other and make the most realistic flowers.

Metallic: Good choice during the holidays and a good accent to other ribbons.

Stripes and Plaids: Most often a grosgrain or taffeta. Makes beautiful flowers.

Velvets: Makes gorgeous textured leaves and simple flowers. Let it's nap work to your advantage as it goes from light to dark.

Sheers: Perfect for airy-looking blooms. See page 100 on making your own sheer ribbon.

***Overlap ribbons, similar to double needle zigzag on page 93, combine different types of ribbon to create an interesting look.

***Use ribbon to weave a basket on a project.

***Fold in a rick rack form for an interesting trim.

***Ribbon looks great on hand bags, children's clothing, pillows for the home and more.

Button, Button, Who has a Button?

ANSWER: I do!

Hundreds of them. I went on a button search several years ago and had a great time. If you frequent estate auctions and antique stores, look for jars of buttons. Look for shops in very small towns, often that is where you can really find treasure. Another great resource is quilt show vendor malls, booths that carry antique fabric, linens and quilts.

When you shop at a top scale fashion fabric store, look for their button department. Often you can find bags of discontinued designer buttons at a good price. Once in Memphis, I found a basket of high dollar buttons for twenty five cents a piece.

Once you catch the "button bug", you will have a wonderful new hobby.

A simple idea for a button project is to cover the collar of a vest or jacket with all types of buttons. This takes a while, but well worth the effort and it shows off the beauty and design of old and new buttons. Buttons are also great accents for the centers of yo-yos.

One of my favorite embellishments is a button bouquet. This is an assortment of buttons, beads, charms,

pearls etc. clustered together to create an embellishments for wearables. I stitch the buttons, beads, charms and pearls on by hand using quilting thread. It is strong and will not break with wear. If a button is large and wants to wobble, use a little glue to hold it in place. To add surprise on a shoulder button bouquet, allow beads t to trail over onto the back of the garment. An examples of this is the top right picture. On this bouquet, black onyx beads trail over onto the back shoulder area. This bouquet adorns "Out of Africa" on page 46. The middle picture is from Sands of Time, Silk. on page 53, a cluster of buttons and pearls.

To the left is a grape cluster created with shirt buttons on "A Vest for Every Season", on page 53.

Beads and Pearls

Bead Clusters

There are so many beautiful beads and pearls available; interesting shapes and gorgeous colors.

I discovered a simple little trick when I made Summer Sand on page 54. Place a small amount of Aileen's Jewel It (dime size mound) on a designated spot. Next fill a 1/2 t. measuring spoon half full of colorful, small glass beads. Carefully turned the spoon of beads over on top of the glue, wiggled it around a little and then pull the spoon away from the mound. Let the glue try and it looks like you worked long and hard, stringing & sewing an assortment of beads.

These clusters make beautiful centers for yo-yos and folded ribbon flowers, see page 100.

I suggest you practice on a sample.

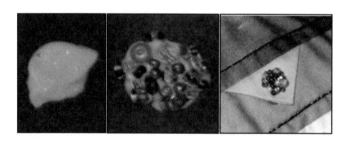

More Bead Tricks

A Sprinkling of Beads

Here is a little trick I discovered at the Houston Quilt Festival. I purchased a beautiful yo-yo vest made from silk fabrics. The woman selling the vest was wearing one and her's shimmered. It had little glass beads all over the front; it was beautiful! Wow!

It appeared she had sewn each of those little beads on by hand, but to my delight, she had glued them on. She put small areas of glue on most of the front yo-yos and then pressed glass beads into the glue. Needless to say, after the glue dried, it looked as if she had hand sewn the beads.

Sewing Beads on by Machine

Small beads of all sorts can easily be sew on your project with your sewing machine with a size 8 machine needle. This takes some practice. Use narrow nose tweezers to hold the bead, sew beads carefully and slowly using nylon thread.

Often beads and pearls come pre-strung on a reel. Use nylon thread in your machine and zigzag a string of beads or edge stitch with a serger.

Swirls of Beads

Clusters of seed beads as illustrated above can applied with Aileen's Jewell It. Place your project on a large table. A pool table works well because the outside rim helps contain the beads.

Place swirls of glue on the project. Use a small spoon to carefully apply a mixture of different seed and larger beads. Lightly press beads into glue. This is a messy job, but worth the effort. Plan to have lots of stray beads, it's the nature of the beast. Stray beads roll much easier on hard surfaces, try to find a rough fabric surface, it will help you corral the stray beads. See picture of Emerald Isle on page 53.

Who has thousands and thousands of Beads?

Answer: I do!

Ok, ok, so I have a new "embellishment best friend". Beautiful gorgeous beads and not the kind you would glue onto the garments. I will always use the Aileen's Jewel It glue trick, but it has been fun to learn the finer art of hand beading. I am very new to this, but have enjoyed learning this art and applying it to my garments.

My first *real project* was the evening gown of "from Nebraska with Love". Swarovski crystal beads and bugle beads were used to create medallions around the scooped neck. Detailed information on these medallions is on page 76.

My most recent project was the ensemble I wore for our son's wedding. It was very simple, but very elegant. The dress was a long, sleeveless, princess style sheath with a scoop neck. It was made of a butter yellow satin with muted rose motifs. Over this I wore a wonderful butter chiffon duster. The exciting part of this ensemble is the yoke of the coat. It was made with confetti fabric, using many soft yellow fabrics, then embellished with stipple bobbin work, using butter pearl cotton. A rose appliqué in butter is on center back. I splurged on the beading for the yoke. Five millimeter Swarovski crystal and six millimeter fresh water white pearls were hand stitched in a beautiful design. See page 106 for a picture of "Soft as Butter" and the back yoke. Oh dear...,I think this is going to be another addiction. Thank goodness my addictions are fabrics, trims, buttons, beads yadda, yadda, yadda, and not nasty stuff.

There are many great artists today who have developed great techniques and applied beading to many different art media. Because of my association with the Bernina Fashion Show, I have come to know a woman who is one of the best in the field of innovative and creative beading. Her name is Larkin Van Horn. We were "sisters" in the 02 show as both our garments were prize winners. The following is information that Larkin shared on a wearable list this last year. I thought it was very concise, a good summary if one were interested in learning this art. I want to thank her for allowing me to print her information.

Beading on Garments and Quilts
By Larkin Van Horn

Supporting The Work

Glass beads add weight to a project and that weight needs to be supported. Quilts have batting that will serve this purpose. For garments, you can use muslin, batting, flannel, or interfacing. I prefer not to use fusible interfacing as the "glue" drags on the thread and can increase shredding.

Needles

I prefer the short beading needles, sometimes called "Sharps", size 10, 11, or 12. You might find the longer beading needles useful for making fringe. The higher the number, the smaller the needle. Size 10 is relatively easy to thread, but may not go through every bead. Size 12 will go through most beads, but is harder to thread.

Thread

I use either Nymo "D" or Silamide "A" for beading on fabric, and always use a doubled thread. Both are nylon - Nymo is flat, Silamide is round. Silamide is also waxed. When cutting the thread off the spool, give it a strong tug, which will help eliminate the curl. If your hands are dry, Nymo will tend to catch and shred. Greaseless hand cream will help.
Thread source: www.Beadcats.com

Checking Beads for Color-Fastness

If the item you are beading will get a lot of wear, you don't want the beads to lose their color. For this reason, you want to avoid dyed or galvanized beads. (Plastic beads can also be a problem if the item is ironed.) If you aren't sure whether a bead will bleed, you can check by putting some acetone nail polish remover on a paper towel. Drop on a few beads and run them

around. The most likely colors to be dyed are hot pink and royal purple. Beads that have a highly metallic appearance can be checked by rubbing with fine sandpaper. If the finish comes off, you may want to rethink using them.

Reference Books:
Bead Embellishment - Robin Atkins and Amy Clarke
The Beader's Companion - Judith Durant
    and Jean Campbell
Off The Beadin' Path - Nancy Eha
Bead Embroidery - Valerie Campbell-Harding
    and Pamela Watts

Larkin Van Horn is an award-winning mixed media artist and teacher, specializing in wearable art, art quilts and beadwork.
Her website is: http://www.larkinart.com

Jewels

Every woman loves jewels and for gala dressing, nothing is more bright and beautiful! Jewels are available in a variety of shapes and colors and well as methods by which they may be applied to your wearables. They are available with pronged sets, with holes to be sewn on and ones that must be glued on.

I used the glue method for the first time with "Starlight Rhapsody", which can be see on page 75. It with embellished with 450 topaz colored jewels. After a year of travel; being packed and unpacked, the jewels were still intact. Nine years later, it is going strong.

The glues made for jewels, such as Jewel-It really do their job. Apply the glue according to bottle directions. If applying to non-porous materials, use either the sew on or pronged set jewels. The glue may not adhere to this type of material.

Swarovski Rhinestones

See page 76 for a close up of "Diamonds"

Over time I've embellished with rhinestones on garments, but always the synthetic or glass ones. Maybe it can be called "evolution" of thinking and design, but after using Swarovski crystal rhinestones, I cannot imagine using anything else. They have so much fire and such beauty.

During the process of designing "Diamonds are a Girl's Best Friend" I knew I wanted to include rhinestones in the design. The cost of the garment was getting higher and higher because of the Dupioni silk I purchased for the coat. I searched the internet for different sites where they could be purchased and noticed cheaper but not inexpensive Czech stones. I mulled this over for a long time and decided "Diamonds" had to have the best, so I purchased Swarovski. There is a difference when the stones are viewed side by side.

I decided on rim sets instead of the prong style set. I was concerned that the prongs, because they come up and over the stone on the outside of the garment, that they would snag the light weight fabric of the evening gown. It took searching but I finally found rim sets. I would purchase them again, they really set off the stones.

I applied the stones by hand, the tool was too expensive. I used a thimble to fold the prongs on the inside. There are 900 rhinestones on "Diamonds", including the dress and coat.

I just have to ask: Where you there?..... Did you see it on the runway in Houston, Chicago or Portland? Along with the rhinestone jewelry and tiara, "Diamonds" was sparkling like fire under the runway lights. A fitting finale

Charms

There are a tremendous number of charms on the market today and they are great embellishments for Wearables. My pattern, Starlight Rhapsody Christmas jacket was designed with areas for charms and jewelry. I Love Santa, a darling Christmas jacket has clusters of charms, highlighting the country look of Debbie Mumm fabrics. Charms can be glued on with Aileen's or sewn with hand quilting thread.

I Love Santa, page 46.
Starlight Christmas jacket page 105.
Emerald Isle page 53.

Jewelry

Lapel pins, old and new make wonderful embellishments for garments. I have a number of bug, bee and lizard pins that I wear on my shoulder and upper back. Placing jewelry in appropriate but unexpected places can add interest to your garments and not just wearable art. It's a nice little visual surprise for other's when they see it.

If you have a wearable art vest or jacket with a beautiful star block on the back, place a pin in the middle of that star, and you have instant embellishment. This is how I embellished the back of Starlight Rhapsody Christmas jacket on page 105. With the added sparkle, people are sure to look twice!

Prismatic Foil

It is so much fun to make new discoveries. I was introduced to prismatic foil when working on "Starlight Rhapsody", my 94-95 Fairfield Ensemble. See page 75 for close up pictures detailing the foil.

It is a paper product, used mostly over the years for auto striping. Basically it's a sandwich of products. A top layer of foil, sticky residue and a layer of paper. It works well for appliqué and it can be pieced into blocks using a straight set. It will not work for set-in points or any place where the foil must bend. Prismatic Foil comes in many designs and a rainbow of colors.

Remember the following when sewing with Prismatic Foil:

#1 - Use a Size 12-14 machine needle.

#2 - In general, small (averaging 3" x 3") pieces move better with the wearer than a few big ones.

#3 - You must use Sewers Aid or other liquid silicon product on your machine needle. There is a sticky residue between the foil and the backing paper. The silicon prevents this residue from gumming up your machine needle.

#4 - Whether using straight stitch or zigzag, stitch length should be a little longer than what you normally use, so that the perforations that the needle makes in the foil are not too close together, so to cut the paper.

#5 - Foil and seam allowance must lay flat, no curves

#6 - Prismatic Foil is Washable.

Glitzy Chicken page 54.
Joseph's Jubilation, page 75.

Rope and Woven Braid

Because of the big interest today in home decorating, there is a great selection of woven braids on the market. Braids are available in a wide range of colors and styles.

These are fun to use as embellishments on your wearable art. I suggest you check fiber content when purchasing and please remember to preshrink your fabric.

"These Boots are Made for Walkin" can be seen on page 106. The focal points on this jacket are boot blocks. When I first saw this block, I knew something fun could be done with it. "Boots" is the outcome. A small gold chain and star charm, representing spurs, embellish the boots.

The jacket is embellished with with gold woven braid and gold rope that encircles the sleeve. It ties at the top of the sleeve and the ends hang loose. It symbolizes the rope horseman use to rope horses.

"Out of Africa" can be see on page 46. The focal point of this vest is the safari tapestry fabric. Different types of woven braids were stitched between the strips of suiting and corduroy fabrics.

The frog closure on "Joseph's Jubilation" in the middle of page 116 is made from a black woven braid. On page 118 are instructions for Chinese ball buttons. I made this type of button using woven braid, they turned out very nice.

"Starlight Rhapsody" on page 75 has 60 yards of narrow gold braid, outlining the major detail on the garment.

The biggest selections for braids, ropes etc., will be found in larger full-line fabric stores with a large home decorating department. Check out the tassels and rayon

Fabric Paint

If you're looking for a great embellishment that's easy and fast, then fabric glitter paint is an idea for you.

Several years ago I made a Christmas vest made from a large poinsettia print. To highlight the flowers and other design, I painted a wash of glitter paint. Red on red, etc. Place a small amount of paint in a container and add water & mix until it is milky looking. The glitter will float on the top of the mixture. Lightly brush this mixture onto the design. When it dries it will leave behind the glitter but you will still see the fabric design. If painting flowers, add a cluster of seed beads in the center. Page 96. See vest, page 105.

Linen and Lace

There are many beautiful pieces of old hand work available today at antique stores as well as new pieces available at craft and discount stores. These are wonderful to embellish wearables. Don't be afraid to layer them, one on top of the other. After they are positioned just right, you can either stitch or glue them down. If using glue, be sure to use the washable glues available on the market. Next Embellish your Wearable with charms, yo-yo's, tassels, buttons, ribbons, small lace appliqués, silk ribbon embroidery, ribbon roses, old hankies, beads, and pearls.

Jackets - Purchase an inexpensive linen type jacket for a very feminine look, or hunt the second hand stores for wool jackets. Wool jackets embellished in this way have a style all their own. I've seen beautiful jackets made out of old Damask table clothes. A dress bodice or vest works well for this type of embellishment.

Bias Trim

A quick and inexpensive way to embellish a wearable is to make bias trim from your focal fabric. The picture below is on a jacket sleeve. To make my trim, I used a 1/2" bias tape maker. The 1/4" bias tape maker would work as well.

Fabric Flowers & Friends

Picture on page 53.

Yoyos are one of the oldest forms of embellishment. My first experience was when I was about 7, a friend had a little box of fabrics cut in circles. She was making yoyo's. Always having loved anything to do with fabric, I started making them as well. Not sure what our plans were for them, but we made yo-yos.

They are still a fun way to embellish in a short amount of time. In June of 02, I was asked to present a jacket workshop that included yo-yos, I felt the little babies badly needed some pizzazz. I had a beautiful supply of designer yarns available and decided to play with them. The results was spectacular.

Yarn flowers or flower centers

If you are right handed, wrap yarn around your index and middle fingers. Three or four wraps for flower center, more for a flower. For tie, cut 6" length of yarn, place between fingers beneath the wound up yarn as illustrated. Tie tightly around yarn. You can leave yarn folds closed or cut on the folds for a fringy look.

To make flower centers, wrap shorter lengths of yarn. Pull ties down and clip. Next anchor with glue in the center of yoyos or appropriate fabric flowers.

Wrap the same for a flower; except use more ribbon and wrap bigger loops. Try mixing different yarns for a different combination. Tie off as above, then fluff your flower. Bead clusters or a button also makes a nice flower center.

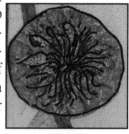

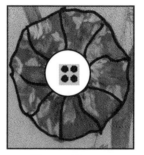

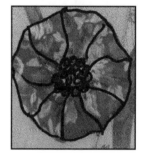

Button Center   Bead cluster center

Ribbon for Special Occasions

Ribbon is easy to make with fabrics such as silk, satins, light weight taffetas and brocades as well as sheer fabrics; if you utilize the rolled hem feature on your serger.

When our daughter was married, we needed a lot of ecru-sheer ribbon; but the cost was prohibitive. One day in Hobby Lobby, I noticed crystalline in the fabric department and realized it was the exact fabric as the purchased ribbon. The "old brain" started to click and I decided I could make my own. I made about 40 yards of ribbon for less than $12.00. It was time consuming, but it was worth it in the end.

To make the ribbon cut the fabric 1/4" wider than the desired finished width to allow for waste when the fabric is trimmed while you stitch. Rayon thread works well in the loopers because of it's sheen. I cut the fabric across the 45" width in 3 1/2" wide strips with my rotary cutter. If longer strips, are needed, cut the strips the lengthwise grain and if you need a really long strip, sew strips together with a French seam.

Adjust your machine, thread and start a running stitch. Check the tension. Sew on scraps of ribbon fabric first to check quality of stitch. Different weight fabrics will behave differently.

As you sew, insert narrow gage wire or fishing line into the rolled hem as you stitch to make wire edged ribbon. Place the wire/line to the left side of needle and pull slightly to left to keep away from blades. Stitch and the wire/line will be pulled into the chain stitch. As you start the hemming process be sure that you allow for the small lip of fabric to the right of the blade to trim so to get a nice roll. Use a short stitch length. If the fabric is light weight, it may try to draw up or ruffle. Place your left hand behind the serger to keep the fabric taunt as it goes through the machine, pull gently in front as well.

The following picture is the bow on the flower girls dress. With fishing line in the rolled hem of the ribbon, there was no problem getting the bow to stand up straight.

Loose Appliqué

My Secret Garden page 106
Starlight Christmas Jacket page 105

Loose appliqué gets it name because the appliqué piece is not sewn down but loose around the edges. I designed "My Secret Garden" for an earlier Hoffman Challenge and used this technique. My jacket was not the winner, but it traveled with the show for a year.

"My Secret Garden" is an interesting design. The foundation piecing design is attic windows. The window frames represents trellis, inside the window is the challenge fabric for that year, a beautiful butterfly print. Growing in and around the trellis are vines, leaves and flowers. The vines and foliage trail over onto each sleeve, which are also embellished with silk ribbon embroidery, small mother of pearl buttons and beads.

The following is for the very simple flower & leaf pattern that was used for this jacket. The following will make a small flower bouquet.

 # 1. Enlarge the templates, then use template plastic to trace and cut the petal and leaf designs below.

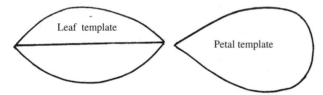

2. Flowers

Cut two 5" x 5" squares of light and dark pink fabric for the flower petals. Trace four petal designs on the underside of one of the fabrics, leaving 1/2" spacing between. Next layer the flower fabrics, right sides together.

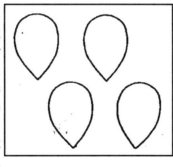

 # 3. Using same color thread as fabric, stitch around each petal design. * To insure sharp points, do not start your stitching at the point, start and end on a straight side.

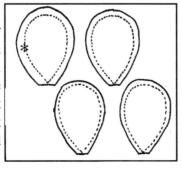

When you are stitching and reach the point, place your machine needle in down position, pivot and continue to stitch. This rule applies anytime you are stitching into a point.

4 - Leaves

For the leaves, cut two strips of two different green prints, each 1 1/2" x 8". Sew these two strips together with a narrow seam allowance.

Cut 1 - 3" x 8" piece of green fabric. Layer the green fabrics with right sides together. On the back side of the pieced green strip, trace the leaf designs lining up center leaf line with seam line.

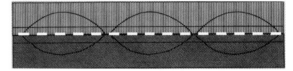

Use same color thread as fabric, stitch around each leaf design. * Read information above about stitching into a point.

 # 5. Cut out designs leaving small seam allowance when cutting. On the flowers decide which side is to be the top of the petal.

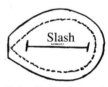

 # 6. On the underside of the petals and leaves, cut a slash down the center as illustrated. Turn each of the petals and leaves, working out points carefully with a straight pin. Place the pin into the point of the appliqué piece and gently pull, the points will pop out. Press well.

Underside of leaf or petal

Cut a small foundation of felt. Spread a thin line of fabric glue along the slash and press leaves onto foundation. Position petals as illustrated and glue them in place the same as the leaves. For petal centers use either a cluster of beads or a yellow button.

If you use this idea in a larger piece, cut bias strips, stitch and turn for stems. Use a ballpoint bodkin to turn bias, press with Celtic press bars.

This technique was also used on Starlight Rhapsody Christmas Jacket, one of my sweatshirt jacket patterns.

102

Embellished Knit Collars

Shimmering Stars Jacket on page 45
Starlight Rhapsody Jacket on page 105
Fabrique Fur Jacket on page 54

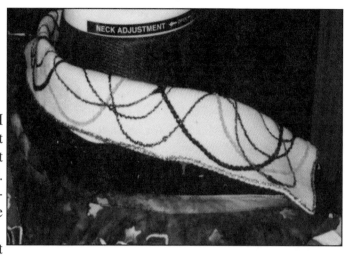

On many of the sweatshirt foundation jackets I make, I add a knit collar. These come in many different colors. After years of using a plain collar, one day it struck me: "why not embellish", so that's what I did. The collar to the right has been embellished with designer threads. Edge stitch along the outside edge of the collar as well and couched in a random manner.

This is fun to do because it's simple and adds a lot to a jacket or shirt collar . Collars can be embellished using a single or double needle along with metallic, sliver or rayon threads. Always start and stop stitching on the neck edge of collar so the raw edges with be on the inside.

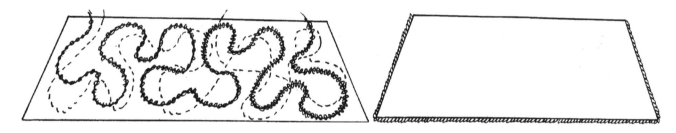

Pieced Collar

Select which collar you want to make. Cut one collar section of foundation fabric. Iron fusible web to the top side of foundation.

Collar A - Piecing starts with #1. Fold and find the center of your collar piece and position # 1 on the foundation piece with the fusible next to the pieced section.. The strips are cut 1 1/2" wide. From there continue to strip piece this section. When you finish adding the strips, trim to fit the collar foundation and press to adhere fusible web.

Collar B - This collar is made of on point squares. Trace your collar pattern onto Pattern Trace. Draw 1 1/2" squares as illustrated below, this will tell you how many 2" squares to cut. Work on getting a good mix of fabric. Consider fussy cutting some of the squares, see page 29 . Sew the on point squares together. Lay the pieced section on collar foundation, press to adhere and trim excess fabric.

Embellishment - Embellish the collar as you wish. Consider machine quilting and designer threads and yarns.

Follow the instructions in your pattern for attaching the collar to your jacket. Remember the collar will be bulky. Be patient in sewing this to the jacket and finishing the project.

Collar A   **Collar B**

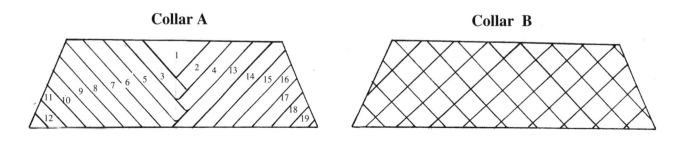

Hand Pleated Trim

There are times when we want trim to match the fabric we are using. Many colors are available but often not the right shade. I had this problem several years ago and this was my solution. I measured the area the trim was to cover. I cut strips of fabric 3" wide, then folded and pressed these strip in half. With my measuring gauge and fingers, I pleated my own trim. I put the strips under the presser foot of my machine. As I stitched using 1/4" Seam Allowance, I folded the fabric in 1/2" Pleats. When you start pleating, use your measuring gauge. After a short time you will be able to eye the measurement, and you will be able to fold and stitch without stopping to gauge.

I don't recommend that you use your machine pleater attachment. When I was experimenting with this idea, I tried mine, but didn't like the results. Making the pleats by hand gives a much deeper and smoother pleat.

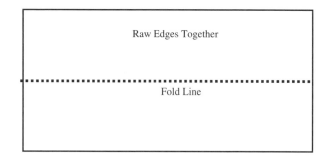

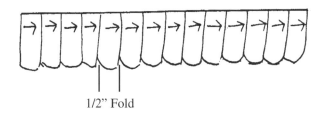

1/2" Fold

Creative Ways to use the Humble Prairie Point.

Prairie points have long been a favorite outside edge trim for quilters. They make interesting embellishments for wearables and other quilted pieces.

Single Prairie Points

Cut and fold squares as illustrated in # 2. A 4" square is a good size for individual prairie points. I suggest lapping these to the center of the next point. You can experiment to see what you like best. Single prairie points can all be made of the same fabric or you can choose many fabrics for a scrappy look.

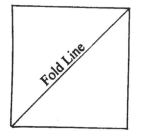 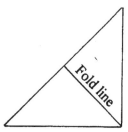 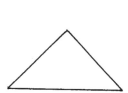

The following are examples of how to arrange prairie points.

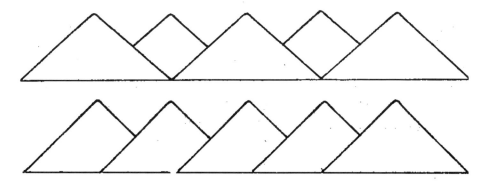

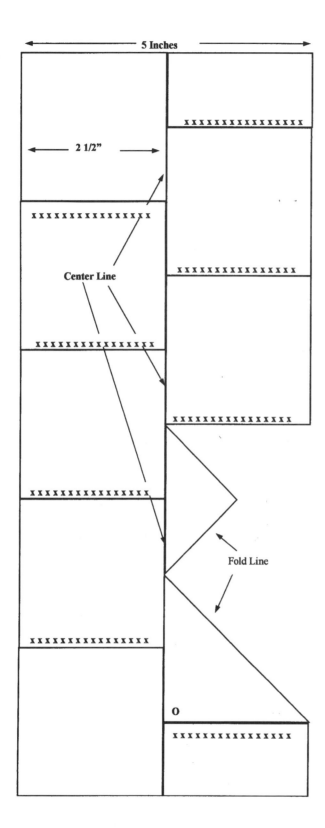

5 Inches

2 1/2"

x x x x x x x x x x x x x x x

x x x x x x x x x x x x x x x

Center Line

x x x x x x x x x x x x x x x

x x x x x x x x x x x x x x x

x x x x x x x x x x x x x x x

x x x x x x x x x x x x x x x

Fold Line

x x x x x x x x x x x x x x x

0

x x x x x x x x x x x x x x x

Draw this onto paper using the above scale, then cut out and fold to get the idea of how it's done.

Continuous Prairie Points

Continuous Prairie Points are a fun and easy embellishment to make. One that works well on wearables. A good size of individual block to used for this trim is 2 1/2" square, that size will be our example. Any size square will work.

1 - Begin with a 5" wide strip of fabric that is the finished length of the amount of trim you require for your project. The half-way point for 5" is 2 1/2". With your quilt ruler draw the center line as illustrated. Using a small Square, mark 2 1/2" Squares along one edge as illustrated. After you finish one side, do the other. Note on the illustration, how the squares on each side, off set one another. Clip along your marked lines (X) to the center line.

2 Now you are ready to fold and press the squares into prairie points as illustrated.

3 - After all squares are folded and pressed, press all points in one direction. Stitch along the folded edge, making sure all raw edges are secure. Your trim is now ready to be applied to your project.

Two Color Continuous Prairie Points

Cut two strips of different colored fabrics, each 2 3/4 inch wide. Sew together with 1/4" seam allowance using a short stitch. Trim seam allowance to 1/8". Press.

Following the illustration make the prairie point trim as you would with a single strip of fabric. If you desire a wider trim, I suggest you play with paper and different size squares until you have the desired width. Remember that 1/4" at the bottom of the prairie points will be enclosed in seam.

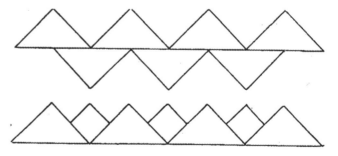

Left Over Diamond

Let's Celebrate Christmas

Curved Seams

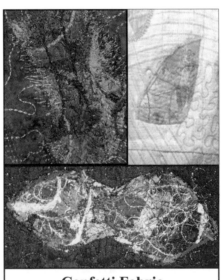

Confetti Fabric

Victorian Lace Vest

Blue Velvet

Star Light Rhapsody Christmas Jacket

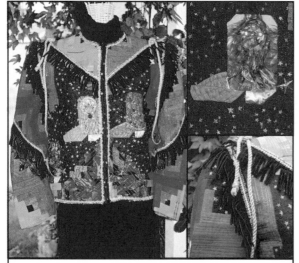

These Boots are Made for Walkin'

Celestial Heavens

Birds of Paradise

My Secret Garden

Safari

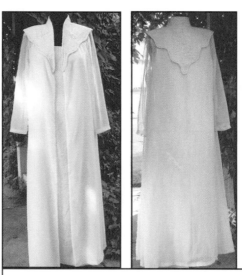

Catch a Falling Star

Soft as Butter

The Finishing Touches...............

Finally we're ready to finish our garment. This section will give you many ideas on designer closures, piping, linings and labels. Almost time for the last good press.

Closures...

Bound Buttonholes

Cut a small section of fabric to be used for buttonholes. Fuse with medium weight interfacing.

A. According to your pattern, measure on garment right front where buttonholes are to be placed. Be careful that the buttonholes are straight. Use a running hand stitch to mark the buttonhole center line as well as the outside lines as illustrated.

B. Cut on grain, strips 1" wide by length of buttonhole plus 1". Fold in half, wrong sides together, then press. Draw a lengthwise line down center of folded strip.

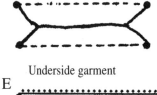

C. Place folded strips with raw edges to the center line, folded edges on outside edge. Baste or pin in place. Mark starting and stopping points. Using a short stitch, sew down marked line. Be sure to start and stop at exactly outside • marking dots. Look underneath to check that the stitching lines are parallel, this is very important to the top side appearance of the buttonhole.

D. When you are satisfied that it looks "perfect", clip open as illustrated. Carefully clip right up into corners.

E. Pull buttonhole strips through to the back side of garment. The small triangle cuts at the end of the buttonholes will tuck right back into place. Pull back the outside edges of buttonhole strips and hand stitch the triangle wings in place. Slip stitch the raw edges of the strips to the interfacing. Press well when all looks just as it should. The outside of the buttonhole should appear as top picture and inside as the drawing to the right.

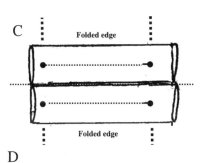

Stuffed Bound Buttonholes

If you are making a quilted jacket or coat, I suggest making "stuffed bound buttonholes".

I developed this technique for Diamonds. Because I wanted to make bound buttonholes, I made several samples to see how my fabric combinations were going to react.

What I found was that a regular bound buttonhole was lost in the quilted fabrics, it needed a filler. I cut narrow strips of batting and inserted them into the buttonholes using my ballpoint bodkin. It took several tries to get them full enough, but they ended up looking much better. Experiment with cable cord and batting as the stuffing and see which one you like the best.

Back Side of Bound Buttonhole

After many years of making bound buttonholes, I decided I did not care for the traditional method of finishing off the facing side of the bound buttonhole. I wanted to try something new.

I suggest you use the same idea as in C, but use a small section of fabric to face this area. Same technique as "buttonhole facing" on next the page. Below is an embellished "back side of the buttonhole" I used "Sand hills Melody" on page 46.

See also Leftover Diamonds on page 105.

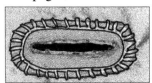

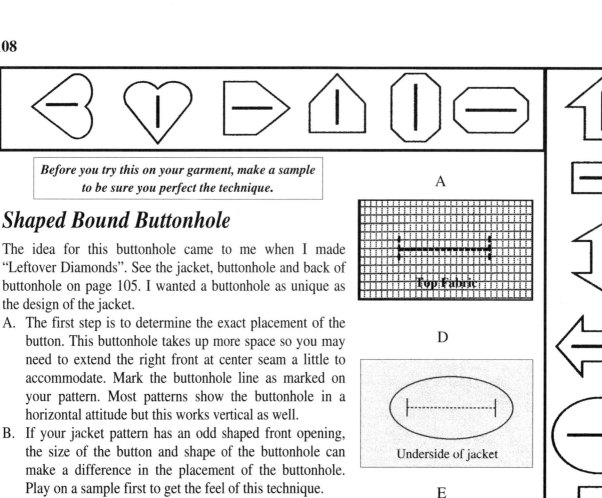

Shaped Bound Buttonhole

The idea for this buttonhole came to me when I made "Leftover Diamonds". See the jacket, buttonhole and back of buttonhole on page 105. I wanted a buttonhole as unique as the design of the jacket.

A. The first step is to determine the exact placement of the button. This buttonhole takes up more space so you may need to extend the right front at center seam a little to accommodate. Mark the buttonhole line as marked on your pattern. Most patterns show the buttonhole in a horizontal attitude but this works vertical as well.

B. If your jacket pattern has an odd shaped front opening, the size of the button and shape of the buttonhole can make a difference in the placement of the buttonhole. Play on a sample first to get the feel of this technique.

C. Measure the length of the buttonhole and buttons. The buttonhole should be a fraction longer than the length of the button. Use a running stitch to mark the placement on your jacket front. Clearly mark both ends. As on A.

D. Select one of the fun shapes for these buttonholes on page 114. Cut this shape out of see through template plastic. On the wrong side position this shape so that it is over the buttonhole marking as illustrated, making sure the size is correct, you may have to adjust up or down. Draw around your chosen shape.

E. Buttonhole Facing: Next for each buttonhole, cut a square or rectangle of fabric 2"-3" bigger all around than the shape. Fuse with interfacing. Position this facing, right sides together. Pin in place. Turn over and stitch from the bottom side, following your markings. Check both sides for accuracy.

F. When you're satisfied, take small, sharp scissors and trim out the center of the shape. Very carefully clip where necessary. At this point, I sharp stitched the facing; you may have to start and stop but this will assure that the facing pulls around to the underside and lays nicely.

G. Pull through to back side. Use fusible web to mesh the facing to the underside of jacket right front.

A

Top Fabric

D

Underside of jacket

E

Right side of facing

Underside of jacket

F

Right side of facing

Underside of jacket front

G

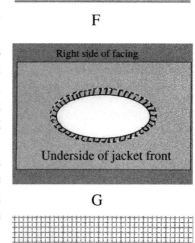

Facing has been stitched & turned

Top Fabric

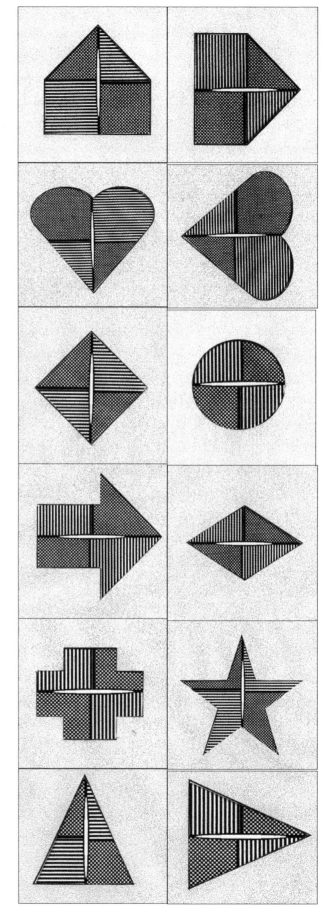

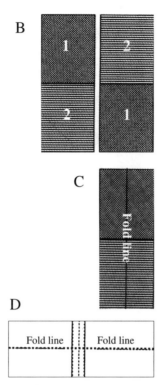

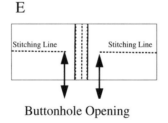

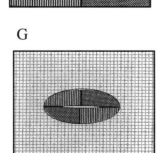

Now what do I do? - Fill the hole!

These measurements are approximate, gauge by the size of your buttonhole. Give yourself plenty of lap room. You can always trim later.

To the right are examples of different shapes and appearances of buttonholes.

A. Apply fusible interfacing to the back of your selected fabric. For illustration cut two 3"x 4" sections of fabric 1, and the same for fabric 2.

B. Next, stitch the sections together using a 1/4" seam allowance. Press open the seam.

C. Fold each section in half lengthwise, press well.

D. Open up each section and place right sides together. Use a pin to match the center intersection of each. Pin and match the fold line on each. Decide the length of opening needed for the buttonhole.

E. Stitch the two sections as illustrated, leaving an opening for the buttonhole.

F. Press wrong sides together for each section and you have the "filling for your hole".

G. Position this section under the shaped facing section of your jacket. Use very small hidden stitches to tack in place around the opening of the shaped facing.

B

| 1 | 2 |
| 2 | 1 |

C

Fold line

D

Fold line Fold line

E

Stitching Line   Stitching Line

Buttonhole Opening

F

G

Another fill idea "for the hole"

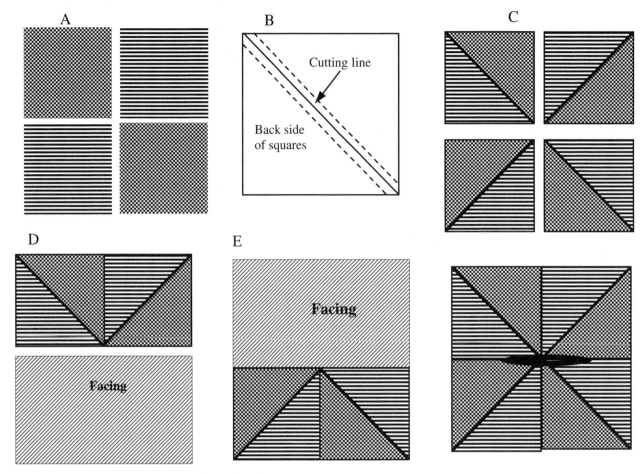

A. Cut 2 - 2/14" squares of two different fabric

B. Place two squares, each a different fabric, with right sides together. On the back side of the squares mark as illustrated. Draw a line from corner to corner. Use an accurate ruler to mark 1/4 out from this line. This will be the seam allowance. Stitch each seam and then cut the sections apart on the first drawn line. Press open right triangle squares, there should be four of them.

C. Arrange squares in a pin wheel design.

D. Stitch two right triangles together using a 1/4" seam allowance. Press seam allowance to one side. Cut two interfaced rectangles to use as facing for each set of two right triangle squares.

E. Use 1/4" seam allowance to stitch facing to right triangle sections. Stitch units together as explained D & E on previous page. Continue with F & G on previous page.

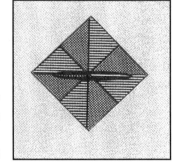

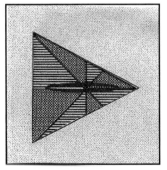

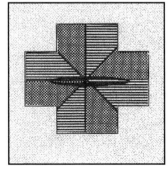

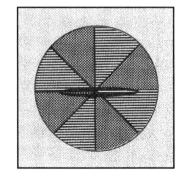

Below are more "fill ideas" for bound buttonholes. The first column is a small black and white check, the second a stripe and the third is pieced. These "fills" would be prepared just as the pin wheel design on the previous page. Do not forget to interface each section of fabric, this will give the buttonhole's a lot of body, which is important so that they "stand up" nice and firm.

There are four pieced sections for each buttonhole in the third column. Each will appear as follows:

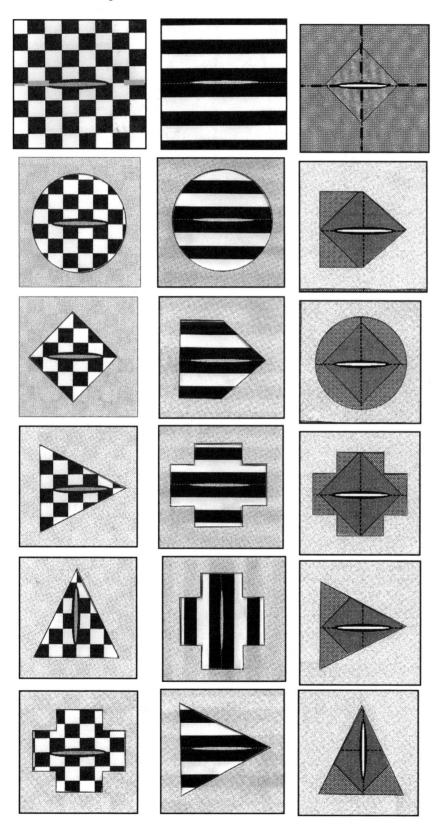

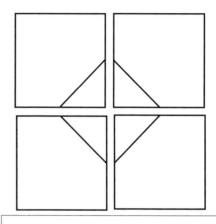

Another Buttonhole Idea

Patch Buttonholes - In a recent magazine I saw a simple, but awesome idea, for embellishing buttonholes. It was a black jacket with a rectangle of fabric about 2 1/2" x 3" that surrounded the buttonhole. Each patch was a different fabric. It appeared that the patches were machined satin stitched in place. The same fabrics were used in the collar and a wide band around the bottom of the jacket and on the dress. The illustration below will give you a good idea of how this was accomplished.

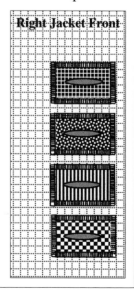

Right Jacket Front

Position of Buttonholes on Different Front Openings...

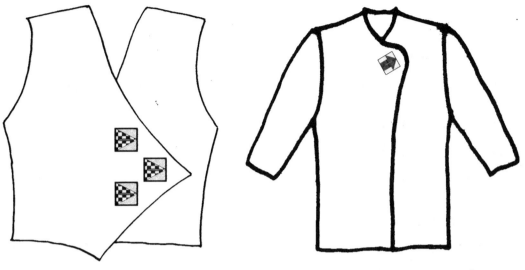

This drawing is of a jacket pattern from Purrfection. With the unusual front opening, it is perfect for a interesting buttonhole.

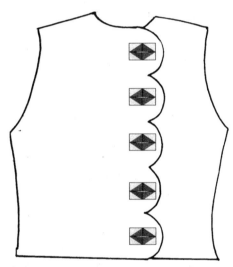

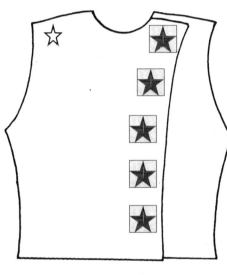

☆ This bodice drawing is how I designed the jacket for "Starlight Rhapsody". The reason I designed it this way, was to allow for as much open design space are as possible. I wanted to use three star blocks on the front of the jacket and still have a nice closure. See picture of "Starlight Rhapsody" on page 75. I did not use the star shaped buttonholes, but I wish I had. How cool!

This jacket is a drawing of "Short and Sassy" by Lois Erickson. I selected this pattern to make "Leftover Diamonds" because of it's great design & style. See a picture of this jacket on page 105.

Because of the pointed shape of the jacket front, I decided to use a round buttonhole. This was to use a different shape to visually make the front opening more interesting.

At the 2002 ASG Conference in Portland, OR, I met a woman who wore a gorgeous suit jacket styled with the same type opening. She made the buttonholes graduated in a triangle shape. The largest button on the outside edge. The buttons were the same style, but each in a different size. It was wonderful!

Being the eccentric person that I am, each buttonhole would have a different button. This woman was a "purist" as I used to be, I am having so much more fun since I have learned to sew outside the box and to make my own rules.

Graduated bound buttonholes.

This is a great style tunic for use with wearable art. There is a problem if you want to make shaped buttonholes. You have to increase the over lap of right front as illustrated by the dotted lines in the drawing. This same adjustment could be made on any jacket with a common front opening such as the drawing below left. Experiment with a muslin for the front opening of all patterns, to be sure of how wide to make the addition.

Double Breasted Jacket opening

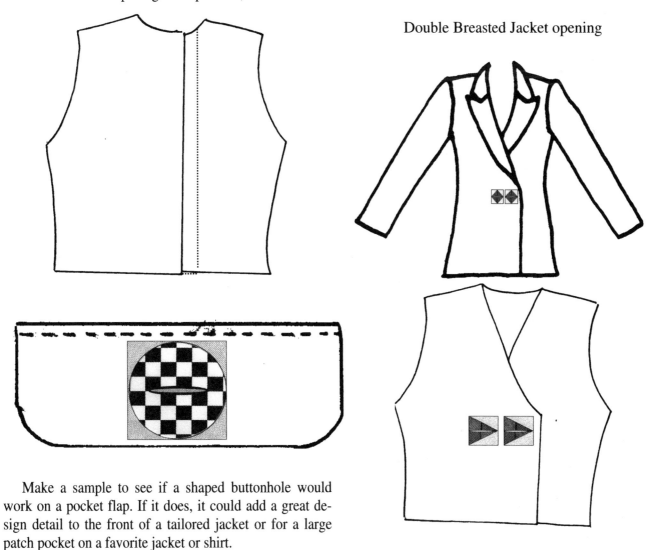

Make a sample to see if a shaped buttonhole would work on a pocket flap. If it does, it could add a great design detail to the front of a tailored jacket or for a large patch pocket on a favorite jacket or shirt.

Templates for buttonholes

Do not cut these templates, use clear template plastic and trace.

Multi Colored Bias Binding, Piping and Closures

One of my favorite finishes for jackets, vest and quilts is a bias binding. The bias strips are cut 2 1/4" wide. Several years ago while working on a jacket, I decided to try something different, bias that included the different colors in the jacket. Thus multi-colored bias binding was born.

Select five or six fabrics in your project, strive for a pleasing mix. The width of the strips of fabric can vary from 1 1/2" to 4" wide. As illustrated, the key to this process is to stagger the strips when they are sewn together. Use the 45 degree angle on your quilt ruler to gauge what the stagger will be with your strips.

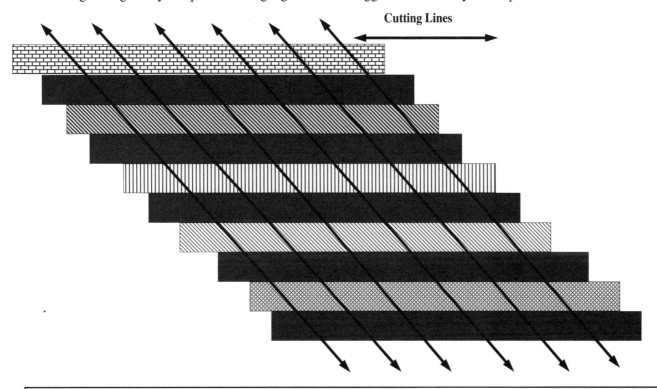

Cutting Lines

Several Suggestion for Multi Colored Bias

Binding on Quilts

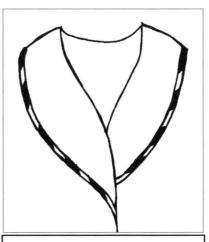

This drawing is an example of Multi-Colored bias used as piping on "Sandhills Melody". Picture on page 46.

This drawing shows Multi-Colored bias used in a frog closure and piping on from "From Nebraska with Love". Page 76.

Bias Frog Closures

Cut a strip of bias about 25" long. This is a great way to use multi-colored bias on page 115. Stitch with 1/4" seam allowance. See illustration on turning bias tube and inserting cord page 14 .

Fold the bias tube in half. Fit the loop end of the fold over the button being used so that you know you will have a good fit for your button. Hand or machine tack to secure loop. Tuck in the ends of the bias tube and finish with tiny stitches.

The illustration below shows how to form the spiral. Start at the finished end of each tube and roll as illustrated below. Pin the frog as you go and then stitch together on the underside with small whip stitches.

When complete, position frog on the right front of your garments. Pin in place and then hand sew in place using tiny blind stitches.

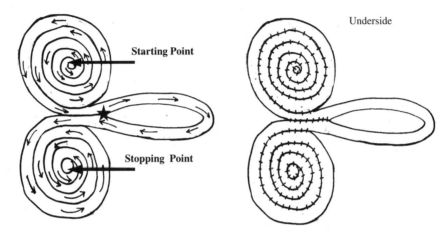

Woven Braid Frog Closures

Frog closures can be made with purchased braided trim. To make, see illustration above. Looking at the picture, the left side is the buttonhole part with the loop, the right side is just two spirals without the loop to give a balanced look. This closure is on "Joseph's Jubilation" 1995 Fairfield Fashion Show Ensemble. Page 75.

Front Closure Extender

The fun part of being creative, is adding to or taking away from a given design. A great addition could be an interesting front closure to your jacket or vest. Add to the right front and lap over onto the left front. Here are several designs that can be used or you can dream up your own. More details on how to do this on the next page.

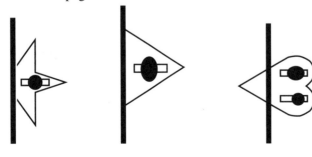

Be sure the size of the extension is as large is you need. Make this addition on the foundation fabric as illustrated. Remember the same modification must be made on the facing of the garment. I suggest that you draw whatever design you want to use as illustrated on the facing, then let this drawn line be your stitching line. Do not cut until after you have stitched, then carefully trim the excess fabric

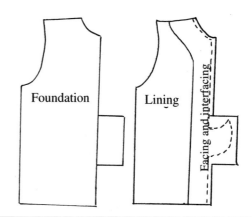

Foundation · Lining · Facing and interfacing

Other Closure Ideas . . . .

Using Design as Closures

This is the front of "My Secret Garden", a jacket made for the Hoffman Challenge in about 1995. It is covered with "loose appliqué flowers and leaves. See pages 101 & 106.

I did not want to mess up the front edges with buttons or a zipper, so I decided to let the leaves and flowers serve as the closures. Small snaps were sewn on the underside edges of the leaves and flowers that extended over to both the right and left center front. The mates for these snaps latch on the opposite center front. Note the center leaf, you can see the snap on the tip of the leaf and on the edge of the jacket on the other side.

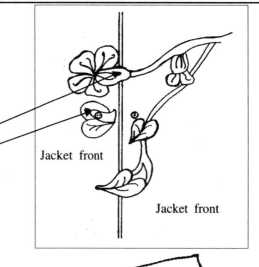

Jacket front

Jacket front

Buttonholes in the Seam

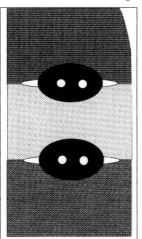

On the example to the left, the buttonholes are part of the seam. On the jacket I made, I designed the center front using 7 different fabrics. So that I did not have to stitch a button hold in the seam allowance, I left the seam open the length necessary for the button.

Different Color Bound Buttonholes

On the illustration to the right, each bound buttonhole is a different color. Refer to page 107 for information on making bound buttonholes

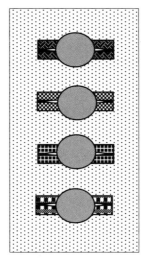

Bias Tube Loop Closure

This is a good closure for a jacket or vest center front that has no buttonholes. It is made from a long, cable cord filled bias tube. See page 14 .

The top end is sewn into the seam; then a loop is formed for the "buttonhole". The bottom end of the loop is hand or machine tacked. Tie several square knots for added interest. I suggest you anchor the lower portion to stabilize. Tack the knots so they do not come untied. This same idea could include more than one loop closure. This idea is from Lois Erickson's "Nomad" pattern.

Buttons. . . . .

Chinese Ball Buttons

These can be made of purchased braid, cording or multi-colored bias over cable cord. Cut a piece of tubing 16" and follow the diagram for the loop formations. Keep tubing seam line on top and the loops open while shaping the button. Draw the ends to pull the loops closer together, easing and shaping the loops to form the button. Pull gently to tighten. Cut off tubing to about 1" on each loose end after the button is made. Pull back bias tube to expose cable cord. Cut off cable cord as close to main button as possible. Place a spot of glue to hold. Fold under ends and stitch securely to the back side of the button. These buttons are large, to be sure of correct size, make a sample. I use hand quilting thread to sew on all buttons.

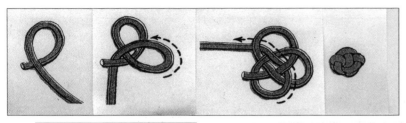

Woven Braid

This was made using a gold and black woven braid. Cut about 22" long.

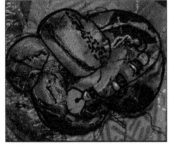

Multi-Colored Bias Button

Use 1/2" to 5/8" cable cord for this button. This button was made using multi-colored bias (page 115) with three colors of silk. Cut strips 2 1/2" wide. You need about 25" of bias for this button. Use soluble stabilizer to couch designer threads down the center of the bias strip. See technique to fill bias tube on page 14. The beads are hand sewn on after the button was made.

Satin Cord Button

Use two different colors of satin cord (rat tail) to make this button. Double the cords so that you have two cords of each color. Cut the cords about 20" long. When you use satin cord to make buttons; use *Aileen's Jewel It* at the point where the strands come out of the button to seal and hold in place. When glue is dry; cut close the extra length of cord.

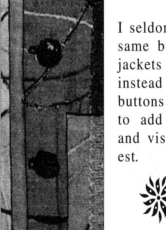

Odd ..

I seldom use the same buttons on jackets or vest, instead various buttons are used to add texture and visual interest.

Rama Buttons

This was one of my "finds" at Quilt Festival in Houston in 01. These are handmade buttons that are fired to this beautiful finish. See page 16 for information.

Covered Buttons

Ideas for covered buttons: cover each button in a different fabric, stencil small designs on fabrics for buttons, machine embroidery small designs, piece in several fabrics. See silk flower button attachments on next page.

I prefer the Maxant brand of covered buttons. The procedure is simple and always works. I interface the button fabric. For durability, before the back is hammered in place, add a dap of hot glue so the back will never pop off.

Silk Flower Button Attachments

Select buttons that blend with fabrics. Use *Aileen's Jewel It* to adhere a small piece of Velcro to the top of the buttons. Make silk ribbon roses. Adhere the mating piece of Velcro under the roses. After you button the garment, mate the Velcro to attach the flower. Push rose down a little with fingers to hide Velcro from view.

Shell and bone buttons

One of my purchases in 2002 was a Dremel, a fun tool for the lady of the house.

Wearable designers can make their own buttons out of Abalone, sea shells, antlers and anything else you can drill a hole through. It is not hard to drill through shell, just slow and tedious. The secret is to keep dipping the shell into a container of water. Keep the shell wet, or it smells like burned bone.

Lining your garments . . . .

Whole Jacket Lining

Use the finished fronts and back of your project as the pattern to cut out the lining. If you do this; the sections will fit perfectly. Place right sides of lining and front, back and sleeves together. Pin and cut.

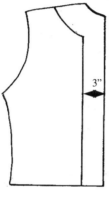

When using this method of lining, the lining is your facing. Trace your garments main pattern pieces; then trace and cut out interfacing pattern pieces. Follow the above illustration and do the same for the back.

When you use this type of lining, you must use bias binding to finish the outside edges.

Measure the outside distance of your jacket and cut this amount of 2 1/4" wide bias. Start sewing the bias near lower center back. When the garment wont' be entered in a show; I stitch the bias on the back side first, then turn to the front and machine stitch in place. Stitch very straight and close to the edge. See information on optional multi-colored bias on page 115. .

Jackets with Facings

When your pattern includes facings and lining, follow the instructions in your pattern.

Envelope Lining for Vest

I seldom use this type of lining; but decided to on "Out of Africa", page 46.

Stitch the side seams of your vest, leaving shoulder seams open.

On the lining, (a) stitch one side seam closed. (b) On the other seam; stitch 3" down from the top and 3" up from the bottom, leaving an opening for turning. Press open seams, as illustrated. Press 5/8" seam al-

lowance to the inside of the shoulder.

Lay right sides of lining and vest together, pin together. Stitch around edge of vest and arm hole with a 5/8" seam allowance. Trim seam and clip curves, be careful not to clip through stitched seam.

Reach through the open lining side seam and pull vest through to right side. Take time and use your fingers to smooth out the edges. Pin baste; then steam press well.

Pull back the pressed lining shoulder seam allowance, pin out of the way. Pin and sew the shoulder seams on the vest, be careful to not catch lining. Use paddled sleeve roll to press open shoulder seams Trim excess vest shoulder seam allowance, then slip the raw edges of the seam under the lining seams. Hand sew the shoulder and side seam lining closed with a blind stitch.

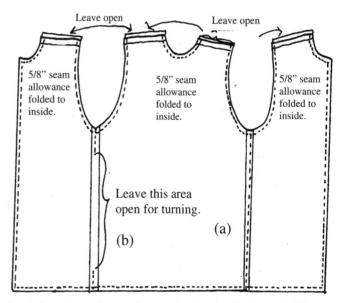

Look for silky prints during a sale, they make beautiful lining fabrics. Try a different color fabric for each lining section.

Designer Lining Finishes

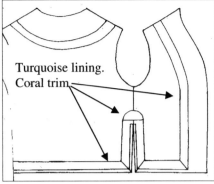

Turquoise lining.
Coral trim

Lining Trim

This lining and trim was used on a silk tunic. The lining is turquoise. The facing is the same silk as the tunic with a 1 1/2" wide coral band added as an accent on the outside edge. This took a lot of time, but was worth the effort as it turned out to be a great finish. The corners were mitered and a half/circle was created at the top of the split. A butter tub lid was used as the template for the half circle.

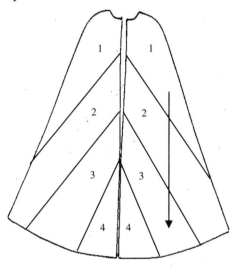

The lining illustrated above made from 4 different fabrics. This lining idea was used on my Fairfield Ensemble "Joseph's Jubilation". 1 purple, 2 fuchsia, 3 teal and 4 gold. It took many yards of fabric because each section was cut on grain as illustrated. See page 75.

Edge stitch the facing on a jacket next to the lining for a nice finishing detail.

Bias Insert

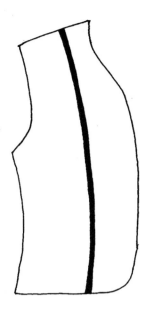

On the lining illustrated to the right, a small folded bias strip was sewn in the seam between the facing and the lining fabric.

I used this technique on "Sand Hills Melody" on page 45. The lining is camel with a lime green bias insert.

This technique was used on "Diamonds are a Girl's Best Friend". The facing is black Dupioni, stipple quilted with red pearl cotton. The bias insert is red Dupioni and the lining is black satin that was random stitched with a twin needle and red Holloshimmer thread from Sulky. See page 91 for more information. See page 76 for color pictures of "Diamonds".

Signature Designer Linings

You can create your own designer lining with the use of a personalized fabric stamp. Information can be found on this sight. http://www.purrfection.com/Click on Stamps– go to bottom of page. Click Custom Stamps.

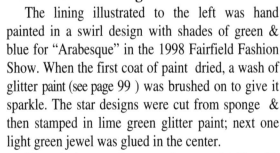

Hand Painted Lining

The lining illustrated to the left was hand painted in a swirl design with shades of green & blue for "Arabesque" in the 1998 Fairfield Fashion Show. When the first coat of paint dried, a wash of glitter paint (see page 99) was brushed on to give it sparkle. The star designs were cut from sponge & then stamped in lime green glitter paint; next one light green jewel was glued in the center.

The painting was done on a large pool table with plastic drop clothes taped to the table. There's more to this story on page 79. Arabesque is on page 76.

Decorative Stitches Embellish Lining

See page 76 for a picture of the lining of "from Nebraska with Love". It was stitched in a grid pattern using a twin needle, decorative stitches & many different colors of rayon thread. A small design was stenciled in every other grid with a variety of glitter paints. The rest of the story on pages 80 & 82.

Label Ideas . . . .

A

"Diamonds are a Girl's Best Friend"

Jenny Raymond Gothenburg, NE 2002 Bernina Fashion Show Masquerade

B

Sandhills Melody AQS/Hobbs Fashion Show 2001 Jenny Raymond

C

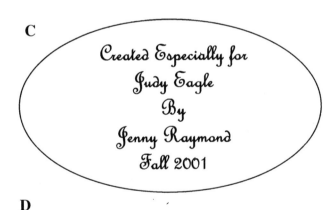

Created Especially for Judy Eagle By Jenny Raymond Fall 2001

D

Sunrise, Sunset

Jenny Raymond Gothenburg, NE

The following are examples of labels that were made for several of my garments. Each was made with fabric that coordinated with the garment.

A. is from "Diamonds are a Girl's Best Friend". It was made with red Dupioni silk with black rayon thread embroidery. Page 76.

B. is from "Sand Hills Melody". A variety of Dupioni silks from the jacket were used. The script was stitched in bright lime green rayon thread. Page 45.

C. was made for a custom order jacket, created with all neutral silk fabrics for a friend in Maryland. Unfortunately, I don't have any good pictures. The label was made from a light flesh silk embroidered in another neutral rayon thread - very elegant & beautiful.

D. is the label for the coat "Sunrise, Sunset" and was made from coordinating solid cottons. Page 45.

Label Lining

For all fabric projects I create, a finished appearance is very important. Labels made for my garments must be "just right", so each one is finished with a lining.

After the fabric has been machine embroidered, I make a template of the desired shape and size of the label using clear template plastic. A line is drawn on the template as a guide, so that I can know for sure that the writing on my labels is straight.

1. Carefully position and draw around the template plastic on the *back side* of the embroidery. Cut a rectangle of interfaced fabric that will be the lining for the label. Place right sides together, turn to label side stitch on the drawn line.

2. Trim the excess fabric and clip the curves if necessary. Make a length wise slash in the lining fabric, then turn inside out. Gently use a pencil eraser to

1
The writing on the label will be up side down.

2
Inside and back of label, cut a small slash.

Facing Fabric

push out the edges out and use your fingers to mold. If the label is square or rectangle, a straight pin works well to work out the corners once the label is turned.

Press and you are ready to blind stitch on your garment lining.

Jeff and Julie Raymond
July 26, 2003

MaKayla Dawn Raymond
Born - May 9, 2003
Daughter of
Sara Marie Raymond

Something special for a family wedding

In July of 2003 our son was married in Colorado Springs. Another special event was to take place one month before the wedding. Jeff's sister Sara and Julie's sister Allyson were expecting babies the exact same date, June 26th.

The March before the wedding, I was on a fabric journey in Lincoln, NE at Hancock Fabrics. My mind always starts to churn in a place such as this and the idea hit me to make receiving blankets for both babies to use at the wedding. I purchased white satin with a small flower motif for the blankets.

Let me go back to the Houston Quilt Festival in 02, where I met a wonderful woman by the name of Linda Dean. She modeled for me at my trunk show, but we didn't stay in touch after the show.....fast forward to Chicago April 2003 and the last day of the Chicago Quilt Festival. Before leaving, I walked once again to the Bernina Fashion Show display to say good bye to "Diamonds". As I was standing there, this pretty lady came around the corner and gave me a big smile. Her face looked familiar but I couldn't think of where I'd met her. It was Linda, we hugged, visited and exchanged email addresses. I've come to know her as a very special woman for many reasons.

Linda is in the machine embroidery business and I asked her to do the embroidery work on the blankets because I knew my time before the wedding, even several months out was limited.

As it turned out, there were surprises from both the babies, our MaKayla Dawn was born six weeks early on May 9th and Zane Jackson Wright was two weeks late.

After Zane's birth, she embroidered the blankets and shipped them to me. She stitched in ivory script on white. What can I say, they were absolutely gorgeous, so beautiful.

A Legacy Tea was schedule the day before the wedding for Julie. Each person was to bring a gift that had belonged to them; something they wanted to pass on to Julie. Because Julie enjoys having friends for tea, I gave her a tea pot from my collection.

After Julie opened her gifts, I announced that I had something special for the babies, to celebrate the wedding and the precious new lives in our families. My gifts were received with love and both babies were carried into the wedding wrapped in their wedding blankets. The occasion made for beautiful pictures and wonderful memories.

If you are looking for someone to do fabulous embroidery work for you, contact Linda at ProSew Embroidery, 8603 Lancaster Ave. Cincinnati, OH 45236 Ph. 513-984-9654 Fax 513-984-6062 prosewshop@cinci.rr.com

Conclusion . . . .

As one travels east to west across Nebraska, a varied landscape is seen. From the Missouri River, to fertile farm land in the Platte River Valley growing fields of corn, high as an elephants eye, one finally reaches the Sand Hills and further west Scottsbluff Monument. This is Jenny's home and she welcomes you to experience the good life of the plains. So much of life has happened to me here and I'm thankful I've been able to live my life in this place.

It's been a real labor of love to rewrite "Creative Techniques for Wearables". I hope that you have enjoyed reading it and that it will be a book you'll refer to time and time again in your "wearable journeys". Thank you for letting me show a little of myself to you, and best wishes to you as you go through the process.

Love, Jenny

Index

Finishing Touches

H

I

J

Retail Order Information

Please check out my web site for a complete catalog of my patterns along with those of other designers. Designer threads and yarns are available as well as knit colors and other notion items mentioned in this book. You can purchase right on line using a secure purchase system.

Jenny Raymond
817 23rd Street
Gothenburg, NE 69138
308-537-3594
Check on web site for current email address.
www.jennyraymond.com